HALLELUJAH

THE POETRY OF CLASSIC HYMNS

1. Hark, how all the Welkin rings
"Glory to the King of Kings,
"Peace on Earth & Mercy mild,
"GOD & Sinners reconcild!

2. Joyful all ye Nations rise,
Join the Triumph of the Skies,
Universal Nature say
Christ the Lord is born to day!

3. Christ by highest Heaven ador'd,
Christ the everlasting Lord,
Late in Time behold Him come
Offspring of a Virgin's Womb.

4. Veil'd in Flesh the Godhead see,
Hail th' Incarnate Deity,
Pleas'd as Man with Men t' appear
Jesus, our Immanuel here!

5. Hail the Heavenly Prince of Peace,
Hail the Sun of Righteousness!
Light & Life to all He brings,
Ris'n with Healing in his Wings.

6. Mild He lays his Glory by,
Born, that Man no more may die,
Born, to raise the Sons of Earth
Born, to give them Second Birth.

7. Come, Desire of Nations, come,
Fix in us thy humble Home,
Rise the Woman's Conqu'ring Seed,
Bruise in Us the Serpent's Head.

8. Now display thy Saving Power,
Ruin'd Nature now restore,
Now in mystic Union join
Thine to Ours, & Ours to Thine.

9. Adam's Likeness, Lord, efface,
Stamp thine Image in it's Place,

HALLELUJAH

THE POETRY OF CLASSIC HYMNS

Foreword by Paula S. Wallace
Preface by Carl P. Daw, Jr.

Edited by Anna Marlis Burgard
Illustrated by Richard Krepel

CELESTIAL ARTS
Berkeley | Toronto

Celestial Arts
Box 7123
Berkeley, California 94707
www.tenspeed.com

Distributed in Australia by Simon and Schuster Australia, in Canada by Ten Speed Press Canada, in New Zealand by Southern Publishers Group, in South Africa by Real Books, and in the United Kingdom and Europe by Airlift Book Company.

Produced by Design Press, a division of the Savannah College of Art and Design
www.designpressbooks.com
Design by Anna Marlis Burgard
Production design by Angela Rojas

"As We Gather at Your Table" copyright © 1989 by Hope Publishing Company. Used by permission.

"Now the Silence" copyright © 1969 by Hope Publishing Company. Used by permission.

"Prayer for Creation" copyright © 2000 by Cathy Yost. Used by permission.

"Precious Lord, Take My Hand" copyright © 1938 (renewed) by Warner-Tamerlane Publishing Corp. Used by permission.

Versions of some images have appeared previously. The illustrations on pages 1 and 67 are based on concept art originally commissioned by Axiom Designed Communications; the illustration on page 30 was originally commissioned by the New York City Ballet; the illustration on page 78 is based on art originally commissioned by Thomson Media; and the illustration on page 102 is based on art originally commissioned by the Johns Hopkins Bloomberg School of Public Health.

Library of Congress Cataloging-in-Publication Data
Hallelujah : the poetry of classic hymns / edited by Anna Marlis Burgard ;
illustrated by Richard Krepel ; foreword by Paula S. Wallace ; preface by
Carl P. Daw, Jr.
    p. cm.
 Includes bibliographical references and index.
 ISBN-10: 1-58761-226-7
 ISBN-13: 978-1-58761-226-8 (alk. paper)
 1. Hymns—History and criticism. I. Burgard, Anna Marlis. II. Title.
 BV310.H27 2005
 264'.23—dc22   2005011985

Printed in China
First printing, 2005

1 2 3 4 5 6 7 8 9 10 — 09 08 07 06 05

For Elizabeth Hyle Burgard, in thanks for filling our home with poetry, and Harald Albert Theodore Maria Burgard, for enriching it with paintings and music.—A.M.B.

For Marcia, my wife, and Jody, my daughter—the loves of my life. —R.K.

CONTENTS

ACKNOWLEDGMENTS

A HOST OF SCHOLARS, editors, librarians, priests, pastors, and friends graciously gave their time, expertise, and enthusiasm to this book as it was compiled and written. The kind souls who guided the work include: Dr. Ysaye Barnwell of Sweet Honey in the Rock, whose knowledge of and feeling for spirituals and gospel music was invaluable; Lily Binns and Jo Ann Deck of Ten Speed Press, who kept keen eyes on the forest when the trees became overly entrancing; Nelle McCorkle Bordeaux, Associate Pastor of First Presbyterian Church, Savannah, who offered suggestions for Scriptural references; David Cusick, former Jesuit priest, current Latin teacher, who helped me wade through the facts of the Latin Mass; Carl P. Daw, Jr., for his generous and scholarly review of the manuscript; Seamus Heaney, for his thoughts on Irish hymns over breakfast in Bologna; Kenneth Woodrow Henke, Special Collections, Speer Library, Princeton Theological Seminary, who went beyond the call of duty in determining the first printings of many of the hymns; Elizabeth Hudson-Goff, for her research assistance as well as fine ears and eyes; Dr. Robin Leaver, Professor of Sacred Music, Westminster Choir College of Rider University, for his criticism and encouragement; Dr. Gareth Lloyd and Dr. Peter Nockles, Methodist Archives and Research Centre, John Rylands University Library of Manchester; Dr. Doris Mack, Director of the Charles Tindley Institute; Marc Nadel, as ever, the shelter in the storm; Dr. Paul Richardson, Professor of Music, Samford University; Angela Rojas, for her patience; Tina Schneider, Reference Librarian, Ohio State University at Lima; Janice Shay, for her support; Jo Trueschler, for a lifetime of mentoring; Paula S. Wallace, President of the Savannah College of Art and Design, without whose dedication and innovative spirit none of this would have been possible; and Hayden M. Wetzel.

I'd also like to extend my thanks to the soloists and choirs I had the pleasure of listening to in Savannah, including those of St. Peter's Missionary Baptist Church, the Cathedral of St. John the Baptist, and the Unitarian Universalist Church for allowing the hymns to live and breathe.

And, of course, Richard Krepel. The first time I saw a print of his work, I was moved to tears by its beauty and subtlety. That I was able to work with him, and on a project like this, seems miraculous. My thanks goes to him for sharing his talent, and for being a pleasure to work with in the process.

A.M.B.

1. Hark,
"Glory to
"Peace on
"GOD &c.

2. Joyful
Join the
Universal
Christ

3. Christ
Christ our
Late in life
Offspring

4. Veiled in
"Hail the
"Pleased as
"Jesus our

5. Hail the
Hail the
Light and
Risen

6. Mild
Born, that man
Born, to
Born, to

7. Come, Desire of
Fix in us
Rise to
Bruise

8. Now display
Ruined Nature
Now in

FOREWORD *Grandmothers and Grand Hymns*

MUSIC IS SO INTERWOVEN with my memories of childhood that the notes of the warp and the visions of the weft readily conjure another place and time. Traditional hymns, especially, circled all around me when I was a young girl, growing up in the 1950s and 1960s—not just in church, but at home, too. And especially in the homes of my two grandmothers, both of whom were pianists.

My Scotch-Irish maternal grandmother, who lived on a farm outside Collins, Mississippi, favored serious tunes such as "The Old Rugged Cross" and "Rock of Ages." There was not much for a city child to do at Grandma's house during the day except fish in the pond, split open an occasional watermelon, and watch her stir the laundry clean in a big black cast-iron pot perched over a fire in the backyard. May Olive Keys Lewis wore simple, practical clothes, her hair knotted in a bun at the nape of her neck. She made her own sunbonnets and aprons from flour sacks. Virtually every morning of her adult life, she rose before dawn to milk the cows, gather the eggs, and prepare fresh buttermilk biscuits for her family. Grandma's small white clapboard church, Ora Baptist, was as unadorned as she was. After one particularly repetitive fire-and-brimstone sermon, I heard her remark, "I don't believe either Miss Ida (her neighbor) or I have sinned enough to need that!"

My paternal grandmother, Gertrude Grace Paul Poetter, lived in Atlanta, Georgia, although she frequently reminded her grandchildren that she was actually descended from French royalty. She never considered herself old enough to be a grandmother, so my cousins, sister, and I were all instructed to simply call her Gert. A former nightclub singer, Gert traveled by railroad all over the United States, alone, until she was eighty. She doted on her pet monkey and a series of felines, all of whom were named Kit Kat. Her favorite hymn was the melodically poignant "In the Garden." (She also tinkled the ivories with "Begin the Beguine" and "The Charleston.") A Christian Scientist, Gert never attended church, as far as I know, but she did have a strong religious faith, unconventional though it was. Her birthday was on Christmas Eve, and that occasion provided the opportunity for an annual family get-together when carols like "Silent Night" and "Away in a Manger" were standard fare. She always said that she didn't want gifts; she only wanted love.

As dramatically different as my grandmothers were, they had one thing in common. They both loved to play and sing "Amazing Grace," though it is most beautifully performed on bagpipes.

Hymns form a tapestry of meaning and memory. Now, then, and forever. Amen.

Paula S. Wallace
President
Savannah College of Art and Design

PREFACE *Songs for the Journey*

GIVEN ALL THE KINDS of poetry and music that currently exist, what is a hymn anyway? And why are hymns important to know about and to cherish? One of the bedrock definitions comes from Saint Augustine's *Commentary on the Psalms,* where he writes about Psalm 148 (as paraphrased by Louis F. Benson): "A hymn then contains these three things: song, and praise, and that of God. Praise then of God in song is called a hymn." Despite its clarity, this fourth century definition excludes much that we would consider legitimate hymnody today. For example, what if the text is petition or lament rather than praise? What if it is exhortation to those who are gathered for worship?

In the last century, another definition was offered by Carl F. Price, our first president of the Hymn Society:

> A Christian hymn is a lyric poem, reverently and devotionally conceived, which is designed to be sung and which expresses the worshipper's attitude toward God, or God's purposes in human life. It should be simple and metrical in form, genuinely emotional, poetic and literary in style, spiritual in quality, and in its ideas so direct and so immediately apparent as to unify a congregation while singing it.

This is a bit more elastic than Saint Augustine's dictum, but many of the terms it employs—emotional, poetic, spiritual— are rather vague. Perhaps hymns are ultimately one of those phenomena of life that we understand better by metaphor than by definition. Consider, for example, the helpful imagery used in a lecture by Archbishop of Canterbury Rowan Williams (then the Archbishop of Wales) at the great National Eisteddfod at Denbigh in 2001:

> Christian song, then, exists in part to give a map of the landscape of faith. It sets out the direction in which all believing life is going—towards God; so it needs to find vivid and forceful language to express why the journey is worthwhile and why those on the journey are passionately committed to it.

Like many maps that are carried in our heads rather than in our pockets, hymns often guide us best when they are most internalized. As we move further into a new millennium with many uncertainties, it is more important than ever to renew our sense of purpose and direction through these sung maps of the landscape of faith. Though our language may fail us in defining them, our experience validates their worth, and that is enough to know.

Carl P. Daw, Jr.
Executive Director
The Hymn Society in the
United States and Canada

INTRODUCTION *Breathing Towards Heaven*

In the beginning was the Word, and the Word was with God, and the Word was God.
—John 1:1

SOME OF THE WORLD'S LOVELIEST POETRY rests within the lyrics of hymns. Since bards first spoke their verse and priests sang their epic hymns, poetry has mirrored our secular and sacred beliefs. From baptisms to funerals, from prayers for peace to thanksgiving for blessings, hymns offer us a literary means to commune with God, and with one another.

THE ANCIENT HYMNS

The inspiration to lift voices in praise spans thousands of years, bridging continents and cultures and creeds. In civilizations as diverse as those of ancient Mesopotamia, Egypt, and India, and, more recently, Germany, England, and the Americas, women and men have artistically expressed their faith by writing and singing hymns to their creators. The word *hymn* is of Greek origin, but what we call a hymn—a song of praise addressing a deity, intended for communal singing—is by no means bound to a European, or even Western, aesthetic.

More than two thousand years before the birth of Christ, the Sumerians—famous for, among other historic achievements, introducing written language to the world—were singing hymns. Enheduanna, a priestess and powerful princess, composed *The Exaltation of Inanna*, a cycle of lyric verse dedicated to the moon goddess. The inscriptions on the sun-baked clay tablets (into which the hymns were carved) offer instructions on how the hymns should be sung and accompanied by the harp.

In Africa, circa 1350 B.C., the pharaoh Akhenaten, Tutankhamen's father, wrote *The Great Hymn to the Aten* as part of a campaign to enforce monotheism across his empire. After Akhenaten's death, Egypt quickly reverted to its worship of myriad goddesses and gods, and even struck the pharaoh's name from their records, but the hymn survives as his legacy:

The birds flutter in their marshes,
Their wings uplifted in adoration to thee.
All sheep dance on their feet.
All winged things fly,
They live when thou hast shone upon them.

Many cultures share this history of sacred song. The Vedic hymns of India form part of the scriptures of Hinduism, the oldest religious texts in our Indo-European pool of languages, dating from about 1000 B.C. There are also hymns by the Greeks (Homer's *Iliad* and *Odyssey,* which were originally intended to be chanted or sung); the Chinese (*Shi Jing* or *Book of Odes*); the Incas (*The Sacred Hymns of Pachacutec*); and, of course, the Jews (the *Torah*).

THE EARLY CHRISTIAN TRADITION

And now shall mine head be lifted up above mine enemies round about me: therefore will I offer in his tabernacle sacrifices of joy; I will sing, yea, I will sing praises unto the Lord.
—Psalm 27:6

In the spring of 1947, Bedouin goat herders in the Judean Desert discovered ancient parchment, papyrus, and copper scrolls wrapped in linen and hidden in clay jars in a series of caves. After further exploration, eight hundred biblical and secular manuscripts—now known as the Dead Sea Scrolls—were found, dating from about 100 B.C. to 70 A.D. Written in Hebrew and Aramaic, the scrolls hold both familiar and previously undiscovered hymns. Poems of adoration, submission, and love for God are found in the "Thanksgiving Hymns" scroll, based upon the Psalms as well as Job, Lamentations, and other books.

In Jewish temple services, psalms were chanted, accompanied by instruments. For the greater part of Christian history, the Psalter, the collection of 150 psalms, was the principal "hymnal" our forebears knew. Not only the content, but also the style of singing is borrowed from the Jews—in particular the responsorial between the priest and the congregation. The first Christians *were* Jews—Christianity was considered a sect of Judaism for decades, one of many in the Roman Empire. As the Gospel was spread and Christians initiated new rituals—including the central sacrament of the "breaking of the bread" now known as the Lord's Supper—hymns not only thanking God, but also praising Jesus, were sung.

The early Christians were persecuted as heretics and enemies of the pagan state. They worshiped and sang secretly, often before dawn in remote locations. But following the pagan emperor Constantine's conversion to Christianity in 312, and the fall of Rome in 476, the faith flourished, and original hymns began to be sung freely during worship. As believers from diverse religious and cultural backgrounds were converted, the message of the hymns helped make the faith uniform, while the singing nurtured a sense of fellowship.

One of the first surviving compositions to be considered a hymn, exceeding a poetic recasting of a psalm, is "Phos Hilaron," a vesper, or evening, song dating from before 400 A.D. *Phos* means *light* in Greek, the common church language of the time, and refers here to Christ's presence in the congregation as symbolized by burning candles and lamps. The hymn is sung today in the Eastern Orthodox churches as well as some Western churches:

Now we are come to the sun's hour of rest,
The lights of evening round us shine,
We hymn the Father, Son and Holy Spirit divine.

In his fourth-century *Confessions,* Saint Augustine acknowledged the growing Latin hymn movement in Italy and the joy this singing offered, claiming, "It was first ordained at Milan that after the manner of the Eastern Churches hymns and psalms should be sung lest the people pine away in the tediousness of sorrow." Saint Augustine also wrote that to sing hymns is to "pray twice," addressing God with public praise as well as private petitions.

In the sixth century, Gregorian chant, named for the school of song begun during the reign of Pope Gregory the Great, was the dominant style of liturgical music. This form of plainchant derives from the unharmonized melodies of Jewish and Greek tradition. During Gregory's reign the church also became exclusively Latin-speaking, after six hundred years of having Greek, the language of the apostles, spoken as well. Greek had become a language of the theologians, and so the switch to Latin, the common language of Italians, was an effort to make the mass accessible.

During the Middle Ages, Latin hymns were written by Aurelius Prudentius and Bernard of Clairvaux, among countless other monks, priests, and poets. These men inked their lyric verse onto parchment and lifted their voices in praise, praying that their words would please the Lord. One of the most famous of these songs, translated in the nineteenth century as "Jesus, the Very Thought of Thee," is a good example of the medieval hymns' artistic merit, including this emotive verse:

O most sweet Jesus, hear the sighs
Which unto Thee we send;
To Thee our inmost spirit cries;
To Thee our prayers ascend.

Latin unified Christians in one language, regardless of their ethnic origins, but increasingly was taught to only the well educated, as Greek had been before it. The mostly illiterate worshippers were left to wonder what was being preached; it would be one thousand years before they would understand their priests, and sing their faith.

THE FLOWERING OF SACRED SONG

And they sing the song of Moses the servant of God, and the song of the Lamb, saying, Great and marvelous are thy works, Lord God Almighty; just and true are thy ways, thou King of saints. —Revelation 15:3

From these Judaic, Greek, and Latin roots, hymnody continued to branch and blossom into a family of song whose members would eventually number in the tens of thousands in English alone. From the Psalms, to paraphrasing of the Psalms, to increasingly poetic works, hymns were sung in church, at religious festivals, and in homes. The next stage of evolution would be their composition in everyday languages, but that would require defiance of the Roman Church, and later the Anglican Church. This rebellion was nothing short of revolutionary. The Reformation led to religious freedoms and innovations, but also to alienation and protracted wars.

Martin Luther is the most famous of vernacular language champions; he opposed any practice or person that separated the individual from the Word of God. An Augustinian monk and priest, Luther suffered over his perceived imperfection as a Christian. After intensive study of the Scriptures, however, he came to trust in grace through faith in Christ's sacrifice alone, not the reliance upon good works and penance that he had been taught were the keys to salvation. Luther wanted other Christians to experience the joy of this prospect of heaven in a language they could understand. To that end, his first original congregational hymn was entitled "Dear

Christians, One and All, Rejoice." He translated the Old and New Testaments and popular Latin hymns into German, just as monks before him had translated the Hebrew and Greek texts into Latin.

English versions of the Bible appeared as early as 1382 with John Wycliffe's handwritten translation, but he and others were martyred for their efforts in bringing the Word to the people. Following Henry VIII's severing of ties with the Pope, and founding of the Church of England, however, there were so many translations that King James called for one definitive edition to be drafted. Forty-seven of the best scholars and linguists of the time were set to the task; the King James Bible was published in 1611. The beautiful language of this work has inspired poets and songwriters, both religious and secular, ever since.

The Psalms are believed to be the work of David, who wrote directly from the Holy Spirit's inspiration. Many faiths maintained, therefore, that sacred song should only be direct or paraphrased versions of what was found in Scripture. To change divinely inspired words was tantamount to sacrilege, but to give new expression to what was already written was permitted. In the sixteenth century Sternhold and Hopkins' *Whole Booke of Psalmes,* or *Old Version,* was the first work that presented the Psalms set to metered verse. At the end of the seventeenth century, Irishmen Nahum Tate and Nicholas Brady published *A New Version of the Psalms of David Fitted to the Tunes Used in Churches,* providing hymns in English that were paraphrases of scripture. This transition toward wholly original

compositions in English opened the Bible to further lyric interpretation.

In the eighteenth century, English churchmen including Isaac Watts, Charles Wesley, and John Newton, moved by the power of their conversions, composed illustrative hymns including "Joy to the World," "Hark, the Herald Angels Sing," and "Amazing Grace." In sharing their interpretations of the "good news" of Christ's message and presence, these poets ushered an emotional element into hymnody. They also broadened the definition of what a hymn could be by writing beyond the confines of strict scriptural paraphrasing, artistically and fervently. They were forced to sing, however, outside the established Anglican Church services, which blocked these masterpieces for the next century. Taught to often uneducated believers in the great outdoors, their hymns were memorized line by repeated line in European and Colonial churches, passed down from generation to generation until they became the standards that are still sung today.

In America, the gospel music of itinerant preachers, especially on the frontier and in southern and mountain territories, developed into a new form of sacred song, witnessing evangelism's concern for the individual's personal experience with God, and public acceptance of Christ into their hearts. But in the midst of these Great Awakenings and their hundreds of thousands of conversions, the national sin of slavery continued. Plantation owners viewed slaves as property, and therefore recognized no human souls in need of saving; the owners who didn't object to mass being said often worked in collusion with the clergy to teach the slaves obedience—that sins toward the master were sins toward the Father.

But through music, the Africans, then African-Americans, found solace. Singing was an integral part of daily life—of work, worship, and social gatherings. While denied their native instruments and robbed of both spiritual and material comforts, they carried to the colonies their religious and musical practices. Their senses of rhythm, improvisation, and of a fully corporal worship style that included dancing and raising their hands to the heavens are a rich and enduring legacy.

As they learned the language of their captors, slaves began to embed messages in original compositions, as when likening their need for release from bondage to the Exodus of the Israelites in "Go Down, Moses." Many were forbidden to congregate and sing, and so would "steal away" to hush harbors—distant fields, or groves of trees far from the overseers' watchful eyes—to worship as the spirit moved them, much as the early Christians did in pagan Rome. These group-authored spirituals or "sorrow songs" began to be transcribed in the mid-nineteenth century, just as the Jubilee Singers of Fisk University toured to help support this university for the newly freed by singing the very songs forged in their captivity. In his 1903 work *The Soul of Black Folk*, W. E. B. Du Bois described this fusion of tribal and Christian beliefs, and song, as the "voice of exile."

The black gospel tradition evolved from a union of evangelical singing's emotional core with the rhythmic and structural heritage of spirituals and modern musical styles like the blues. Influential preacher-musicians like Charles Tindley, the son of a slave, turned the messages of charismatic sermons into powerful and moving hymns. Tindley in turn inspired Thomas A. Dorsey, and from the talents of these two men (whose works include standards such as "I'll Overcome Some Day" and "Precious Lord, Take My Hand") came a revolution in the sound and look of sacred—and popular—music. Sam Cooke, Elvis Presley, Johnny Cash, and numerous others were inspired by gospel songs; many were given their starts as professional musicians performing in church choirs.

After centuries of struggle and hope, the individual's immediate relationship with the Word of God prevailed across all Christian denominations. Catholics had sung hymns and listened to parts of the mass in their native languages for centuries, but saying the *entire* mass in the vernacular had never been sanctioned. In 1965, the Second Vatican Council finally allowed that the liturgy for the Mass could be celebrated in languages other than Latin, and encouraged the use of vernacular hymns. It also permitted greater participation from laity, and in general, as Pope John XXIII said at the Council's opening, "threw open the windows of the Church so that we can see out and the people can see in."

As Luther had turned to the Latin Breviary for some of the first hymns sung in German, now the Catholic Church adopted some of the finest Protestant hymns, including Luther's own "A Mighty Fortress Is Our God."

THE POETRY OF HYMNS

I will pray with the spirit, and I will pray with the understanding also: I will sing with the spirit, and I will sing with the understanding also. —I Corinthians 14:15

The Bible has inspired countless poems, small gleaming gems and grand epics alike. Some—with or without the artists' permission or religious intention—have been paired with musical scores in hymnals, including poems by Christina Rossetti, E. E. Cummings, and Robert Frost. Others, including T. S. Eliot's "A Song for Simeon," Sylvia Plath's "Lady Lazarus," and Langston Hughes's "Carol of the Brown King," allude to biblical stories to convey contemporary human concerns. Simeon, Lazarus, and the Magi are instantly familiar to us; their stories are a sort of literary shorthand, as their plights and triumphs mirror our own. Only a fine line exists at times between sacred and secular works, but hymns must rise from the page as song, maintaining their beauty and strength under the burden of repetition.

Hymns present the Word of God through the words of poets; they silence the hectic world, then reverberate within our spirits long after the last notes have faded. They bind us to our religious forebears, ancestors, and future generations at once, embracing the Gospel as they once did, and as they will.

Isaac Watts once likened singing hymns to "breathing towards heaven," offering our praise to the God that gave us life with his own breath. But when we sing hymns in church, surrounded by our families, neighbors, and choirs, we can overlook the messages that their authors struggled to perfect. We become so aware of our voices, in keeping time and staying on key, that the ideas and emotions we sing recede into the familiar music. Reading the verse in a quiet moment outside of a church setting, on the other hand, encourages a kind of communion with God. Once reacquainted with the original poems, we can "sing with understanding," guided, assuaged, and with our spirits bound for glory.

Catholic, Moravian, Lutheran, Anglican, Baptist, Methodist—these and a host of other denominations have poets who speak to their specific doctrines. But the hymns themselves defy the boundaries of creed, forming an ecumenical fellowship of words as the hymnals for these often fiercely divergent groups, with very few exceptions, share one another's songs. Hymns remind us of our common heritage as Christians— the message of Christ, regardless of disparate interpretations.

The day I was born, my great-uncle, Bishop Hyle, was in Rome as part of the Second Vatican Council. My father's (German) mother was a Third Order Carmelite; my mother's mother attended Billy Sunday's camp revivals. My parents woke us with Gregorian chants on Sundays, and once drove us to New York for the day just to hear Mahalia Jackson sing gospel hymns. Priests said mass for us in our home, and sang with us around the family piano. My childhood was filled with many faiths and many voices. This book is their echo.

Anna Marlis Burgard
Tybee Island, Georgia

STILL THINE ANGELS 'ROUND ME SING
1500–1699

With all my heart I would extol the precious gift of God in the noble art of music... Music is to be praised as second only to the Word of God because by her all the emotions are swayed. —Martin Luther

ON A COLD DAY IN 1519, in a tower of Wittenberg's Black Cloister, Martin Luther struggled with a single phrase from Romans 1:17: *For therein is the righteousness of God revealed from faith to faith: as it is written, The just shall live by faith.* He, like so many believers of his time, interpreted St. Paul's words as a warning that God would punish sinners like him, and this made him angry—how could he ever be faithful or pure enough to be saved? But after months of prayer and meditation, Luther reread, as with new eyes, the end of the passage: *The just shall live by faith.* By faith alone he would be saved; God had *already* saved him through the sacrifice of his son. In that instant of clarity he felt "born again," as if the "very gates of paradise" had been opened to him. This was the moment of Luther's personal spiritual transformation, and the true beginning of the Reformation.

Like many great historical figures, Luther was born at an auspicious time. After fifteen hundred years of conversions, the Roman Catholic Church was the most powerful entity in the Western world. Kings bowed in allegiance to the Church, and filled its coffers with taxes collected from their subjects. This political and financial strength supported many important causes. Beyond the Church's primary spiritual functions, it helped main-

tain order in society and sponsored a true flowering of the arts. Monastic scholars preserved ancient knowledge by transcribing the classics. Fra Angelico, Michelangelo, Raphael, and scores of other painters, sculptors, and architects were offered the means and inspiration to create some of the world's great masterpieces. The church fostered the development of music as its scholars standardized musical notation, and its priests and poets poured out streams of lyric hymns.

But the "priesthood of all believers" had changed a great deal from its humble beginnings with Jesus' Sermon on the Mount. Individuals within the enormous hierarchy of the Church, including the infamous minds behind the Inquisitions and the corrupt Renaissance popes, had brought practices into the church that many found appalling, and far from holy. Voices of dissent were frequently raised from the masses, but were quickly, and at times quite severely, silenced.

Yet the desire for reform prevailed in the face of torture and imprisonment. Luther ushered in an intelligent and passionate protest to a number of church laws and behaviors, aided by the breadth of communication made possible by Gutenberg's printing press. He had not intended to separate from the Church, but rather to make it more pure and inclusive. When no compromise could be reached, however, he and others of a like mind broke free of Rome and founded churches of their own. The Reformation was a pivotal event in history—a series of religious divides marked by protests and persecutions that would affect far more than just how people worshiped God. Through the defiance of a few courageous men, the rights of all believers to participate in the mass were recognized.

Jan Hus, a fifteenth-century priest—and founder of the Bohemian Brethren, which later evolved into the Moravian Church—insisted that it was the right and also the *duty* of Christians to read and interpret the Bible for themselves. He was the first to translate it into a vernacular language, preaching in his native Czech. Luther followed Hus' lead, translating the Latin Bible and hymns into German. Lutherans embraced singing wholeheartedly, offering up both German versions of the Latin hymns and original compositions. Within fifty years, 70 percent of Germans would be Protestant, but of two opposing factions: the followers of the austere scholar John Calvin (who rejected original hymns as blasphemous), and the Lutherans. This conflict contributed to the Thirty Years War, which claimed millions of lives, but even in the wake of those losses, gracious hymns were written. Martin Rinkart's "Now Thank We All Our God" rose above displacement, famine, and disease to help believers forge through sorrow by expressing their love for God and recognizing his greater blessings.

A contemporary of Luther's, the English priest William Tyndale, went into exile to meet with Luther and complete his New Testament, 18,000 copies of which were printed in Germany and smuggled into England in 1525. Just a few years later, King Henry VIII forced the schism from Rome and formed the Church of England. The newly sanctioned use of English translations of the Bible followed, the definitive version of which was sponsored by King James a century later. Hymns by John Milton and Thomas Ken reflected the influence of its beautiful, rhythmic prose.

It wasn't long before the Anglican Church, too, began to splinter. George Fox founded the Society of Friends, or Quakers, who denied the validity of the clergy, liturgy, and sacraments of the mass. Presbyterians in Scotland followed the tenets of predestination introduced to them by Calvin's associate in Geneva, John Knox. John Smith, an Anglican priest, founded the Baptist faith, inspired by the conviction that only those who actively accepted Jesus, not unaware infants, should be baptized. Reformer Roger Williams and Quaker William Penn risked their lives to establish religiously tolerant communities in the colonies. The trade in African slaves also began, which in itself started a new era of oppression. Both immigrants and slaves would lift their voices in song in America, but from very different motivations.

Hymns had lifted spirits and fortified hearts for thousands of years. While most early compositions were paraphrases of the Judaic Psalms, slowly, cautiously, a more original art form developed in the seventeenth century, which helped define the creeds of the emerging denominations.

A Mighty Fortress Is Our God

In that day shall this song be sung in the land of Judah; We have a strong city; salvation will God appoint for walls and bulwarks. —Isaiah 26:1

A mighty fortress is our God,
A bulwark never failing;
Our helper he amid the flood
Of mortal ills prevailing.
For still our ancient foe
Doth seek to work us woe,
His craft and power are great,
And armed with cruel hate,
On earth is not his equal.

Did we in our own strength confide
Our striving would be losing,
Were not the right man on our side,
The man of God's own choosing.
Dost ask who that may be?
Christ Jesus, it is he,
Lord Sabaoth his name,
From age to age the same,
And he must win the battle.

And though this world, with devils filled,
Should threaten to undo us,
We will not fear, for God hath willed
His truth to triumph through us.
The Prince of Darkness grim,—
We tremble not for him;
His rage we can endure,
For lo! his doom is sure;
One little word shall fell him.

That word above all earthly powers,
No thanks to them—abideth;
The spirit and the gifts are ours
Through Him who with us sideth.
Let goods and kindred go,
This mortal life also;
The body they may kill,
God's truth abideth still,
His kingdom is for ever.

Martin Luther Wittenberg, Germany, 1528 *Lutheran;* translated by Frederick Henry Hedge, 1852
These were the words Luther sang in times of doubt; the hymn's lyrics, derived from Psalm 46, echo his description of prayer as "a strong wall and fortress of the church... a goodly Christian weapon." It remains the most popular of all German hymns, sung all over the world by many denominations in many languages, including the Catholic Church, whose practices Luther protested five hundred years ago during the Reformation.

Now Thank We All Our God

Enter into his gates with thanksgiving, and into his courts with praise; be thankful unto him, and bless his name.
—Psalm 100:4

Now thank we all our God
With heart and hands and voices,
Who wondrous things hath done,
In whom His world rejoices;
Who from our mother's arms
Hath bless'd us on our way
With countless gifts of love
And still is ours today.

Oh may this bounteous God
Through all our life be near us,
With ever joyful hearts
And blessed peace to cheer us;
And keep us in His grace,
And guide us when perplex'd,
And free us from all ills
In this world and the next.

All praise and thanks to God
The Father, now be given,
The Son, and Him who reigns
With them in highest heaven,
The One eternal God,
Whom earth and heaven adore,
For thus it was, is now,
And shall be evermore!

Martin Rinkart Eilenburg, Germany, 1636 *Lutheran;* translated by Catherine Winkworth, 1858
Second in popularity only to "A Mighty Fortress Is Our God" in Germany, this hymn has a story which is both tragic and triumphant. The Thirty Years War—a conflict on the scale of modern world wars, with a host of countries defending and attacking the Catholic Hapsburg Empire—was rife with atrocities. During the siege of the walled town of Eilenburg, Rinkart, a musician and poet, served as pastor. Refugees from surrounding villages flooded inside the walls, seeking safety from Swedish troops. In spite of the siege, and though weakened by the famine and pestilence that came with overcrowding, Rinkart's spirit rose above the fray. He maintained his belief in mercy even as he buried the dead, conducting funeral services for as many as forty to fifty people each day—including his wife and some of his children. Written under extreme duress, these lyrics illustrate the strength of faith under the most dire of circumstances.

The Lord Will Come and Not Be Slow

Truth shall spring out of the earth; and righteousness shall look down from heaven. — Psalm 85:11

The Lord will come, and not be slow,
His footsteps cannot err;
Before him righteousness shall go,
His royal harbinger.

Mercy and truth, that long were missed,
Now joyfully are met;
Sweet peace and righteousness have kissed,
And hand in hand are set.

Truth from the earth, like to a flower
Shall bud and blossom then,
And justice, from her heavenly bower
Look down on mortal men.

Rise, God, judge thou the earth in might,
This wicked earth redress;
For thou art he who shalt by right
The nations all possess.

The nations all whom thou hast made
Shall come, and all shall frame
To bow them low before thee, Lord,
And glorify thy name.

Thee will I praise, O Lord, my God,
Thee honor and adore
With my whole heart, and blaze abroad
Thy name for evermore!

JOHN MILTON London, England, 1648

Based upon selections from Psalms 82–86, this metrical psalm was first published in *Poems, &c, Upon Several Occasions* in 1673; it first appeared as a hymn in *The New Congregational Hymn Book* in 1855, more than two hundred years after its composition. With their artistic language surpassing a mere rewording of the Psalms, Milton's hymns are considered the predecessors of those of eighteenth-century hymnist Isaac Watts. Milton is best known as the author of *Paradise Lost,* his epic poem of Adam and Eve's fall from grace, and his defense of the free press, *Areopagitica.* Milton believed in three essential freedoms: religious, domestic, and civil; defending all of these through his writings transformed him into one of the premiere poetic talents of the English language.

It was religious and civil freedoms that led him directly to the frontlines of the English Civil War, during which he served under the Puritan Oliver Cromwell as Secretary of Foreign Tongues. He was imprisoned, escaping execution only when the restored King Charles II released him. His religious beliefs demanded a personal relationship with God, one not filtered through other men's laws or the traditions of priests and preachers. He looked directly to the Bible for hope and a sense of justice. He was against most forms of organized religion, and while he supported the Puritan government, defied religious classification himself. He suffered many losses in his lifetime, including his wife, children, fortune, and ever-failing eyesight, all within twelve years. Progressive and poetic, rebellious and stoic, Milton reflects many of the qualities that have formed the best hymnists before and since. His works and ethics have influenced, among countless others, William Blake, John Keats, J. R. R. Tolkien, and C. S. Lewis.

Now All the Woods Are Sleeping

He shall cover thee with feathers, and under his wings shalt thou trust: his truth shall be thy shield and buckler. —Psalm 91:4

Now all the woods are sleeping,
And night and stillness creeping
O'er field and city, man and beast;
But thou, my heart, awake thee,
To prayer awhile betake thee,
And praise thy Maker ere thou rest.

O Sun, where art thou vanish'd?
The Night thy reign hath banish'd
Thy ancient foe, the Night.
Farewell, a brighter glory
My Jesus sheddeth o'er me,
All clear within me shines His light.

The last faint beam is going,
The golden stars are glowing
In yonder dark-blue deep;
And such the glory given
When called of God to heaven,
On earth no more we pine and weep.

Ye aching limbs! now rest you,
For toil hath fore oppress'd you,
Lie down my weary head:
A sleep shall once o'ertake you
From which earth ne'er shall wake you,
Within a narrower colder bed.

My Jesus, stay Thou by me,
And let no foe come nigh me,
Safe sheltered by Thy wing;
But would the foe alarm me,
Oh, let him never harm me,
But still Thine angels 'round me sing!

My loved ones, rest securely,
From every peril surely
Our God will guard your heads;
And happy slumbers send you,
And bid His hosts attend you,
And golden-arm'd, watch o'er your beds.

PAUL GERHARDT Berlin, Germany, 1648 *Lutheran;* translated by Catherine Winkworth, 1856
Gerhardt, like Martin Rinkart, lived through the German Civil War, a period of embattlement between Calvinists and Lutherans that was part of the Thirty Years War. While the two sides fought for believers and political control, Gerhardt's sermons and hymns were embraced by followers of both denominations, with his church filled to standing room only when he spoke. Even when he was forbidden to preach due to conflicts with the ruling Calvinists, the flock came to his home, and the public fought for their preacher. Gerhardt's hymns were more popular even than Luther's; many attribute this to the positive light in which Gerhardt portrayed God, as loving and kind, whereas Luther's God was more of might.

The tradition of vesper, or evening, hymns evolved from the Judaic practice of beginning day at sundown, which follows the order of creation in Genesis 1:5: *And there was evening and there was morning, one day.* These hymns are thanksgivings for the day that's ending, and a preparation for sleep and the dawn of a new day.

Give to the Winds Thy Fears

Have not I commanded thee? Be strong and of good courage; be not afraid, neither be thou dismayed: for the Lord thy God is with thee whithersoever thou goest. —Joshua 1:9

Give to the Winds thy Fears,
Hope, and be undismay'd.
God hears thy Sighs and counts thy Tears,
God shall lift up thy Head.

Thro' Waves and Clouds and Storms
He gently clears thy Way;
Wait thou his Time; so shall this Night
Soon end in joyous Day.

Still heavy is thy Heart?
Still sinks thy Spirit down?
Cast off the Weight, let Fear depart,
Bid ev'ry Care be gone.

What tho' Thou rulest not?
Yet Heav'n, and Earth, and Hell
Proclaim, God sitteth on the Throne,
And ruleth all things well!

Leave to his Sov'reign Sway
To choose and to command;
So shalt thou wondering own his Way
How wise, how strong this Hand.

Far, far above thy Thought,
His Counsel shall appear,
When fully He the work hath wrought,
That caus'd thy needless Fear.

Thou seest our Weakness, Lord;
Our Hearts are known to Thee;
O lift Thou up the sinking Hand,
Confirm the feeble Knee!

Let us in Life, in Death,
Thy steadfast Truth declare,
And publish with our latest Breath
Thy Love and Guardian Care!

PAUL GERHARDT Berlin, Germany, 1656 *Lutheran;* translated by John Wesley, 1736
Considered the "Poet of the Lutheran Church," Gerhardt believed in a loving God, and that Christians of opposing views should be able to discuss their differences civilly and without reproach, with full freedoms of speech and belief. Through the atrocities of the German Civil War, he stood firm in his faith and aided others through his example and songs. The author of more than 100 hymns, Gerhardt was described as persuasive and devout, cheerful, conscientious, and charitable.

John Wesley translated Gerhardt's hymn while serving as an Anglican missionary in Savannah, Georgia. This and other works appeared in the first hymnal published in America, *A Collection of Psalms and Hymns,* compiled by Wesley. John and his brother, Charles, were deeply impressed by the spiritual fortitude of the Moravians on their voyage to Georgia, as they faithfully and fearlessly sang their German hymns through terrible storms. Both men sought spiritual council from the Moravians before they formed their own denomination, Methodism, after their return to England.

Awake, My Soul, and With the Sun

And that, knowing the time, that now it is high time to awake out of sleep: for now is our salvation nearer than when we believed. The night is far spent, the day is at hand: let us therefore cast off the works of darkness, and let us put on the armour of light. —Romans 13:11-12

Awake, my Soul, and with the Sun
Thy daily Stage of Duty run,
Shake off dull Sloth, and joyful rise
To pay thy Morning Sacrifice.

Thy precious Time misspent, redeem,
Each present Day thy last esteem,
Improve thy Talent with due Care,
For the great Day thyself prepare.

In Conversation be sincere;
Keep Conscience, as the Noon-tide clear;
Think how all seeing God thy Ways,
And all thy Secret Thoughts, surveys.

By influence of the Light divine,
Let thy own Light to others shine;
Reflect all Heav'n's propitious Ways
In ardent love, and cheerful Praise.

Wake, and lift up thyself, my Heart,
And with the Angels bear thy Part,
Who all Night long unweary'd sing
High Praise to the eternal King.

Had I your Wings, to heav'n I'd fly;
But God shall that defect supply,
And my Soul, wing'd with warm Desire,
Shall all Day long to Heav'n aspire.

Heav'n is, dear Lord, where e'er thou art:
O never then from me depart;
For to my Soul 'tis Hell to be
But for one Moment void of thee.

Lord, I my Vows to thee renew,
Disperse my sins as morning dew;
Guard my first Springs of Thought and Will,
And with thyself my Spirit fill.

Direct, control, suggest this Day
All I design, or do, or say,
That all my Pow'rs, with all their Might,
In thy sole Glory may unite.

Praise God, from Whom all Blessings flow;
Praise him, all Creatures here below;
Praise him above, ye heav'nly Host;
Praise Father, Son, and Holy Ghost.

THOMAS KEN London, England, 1674 *Anglican*
This, one of a trilogy of hymns for morning, evening, and midnight, was sung by Ken every day as he accompanied himself with the lute. The last stanza is commonly referred to as the Doxology—one of the most frequently sung compositions of the last 300 years. Ken served as royal chaplain to King Charles II. Under Charles, who respected Ken's forthright manner, he was promoted to the bishopric of Bath and Wells. Unfortunately for Ken, the next—and Catholic—king, James II, Charles's brother, was not so tolerant. Ken was imprisoned in the Tower of London with other Anglican leaders who defied the new king until the people of London rioted for their release. Though Queen Anne later offered to restore him to his position, he refused, and spent the rest of his years quietly as a tutor and poet.

Now from the Altar of My Heart

Let my prayer be set before thee as incense, and the lifting up of my hands as the evening sacrifice. —Psalm 141:2

Now from the Altar of my Heart
Let incense flames arise.
Assist me, Lord, to offer up
Mine Evening Sacrifice.

Awake, my Love; Awake, my Joy;
Awake, my Heart and Tongue.
Sleep not when Mercies loudly call:
Break forth into a Song.

Man's Life a book of History,
The Leaves thereof are dayes,
The Letters Mercies closely Joyn'd,
The Title is thy Praise.

This day God was my Sun and Shield,
My Keeper and my Guide;
His care was on my frailty shown,
His mercies multiply'd.

Minutes and Mercies multiply'd
Have made up all this day;
Minutes came quick but Mercies were
More fleet and free than they.

New time, new Favours, and new Joys
Do a new Song require:
Till I shall praise thee as I would,
Accept my Heart's desire.

Lord of my Time, Whose Hand hath set
New time upon my Score,
Then shall I praise for all my Time,
When Time shall be no more.

JOHN MASON Water-Stratford, England, 1683 *Anglican Independent*
The son of a dissenting minister, and a clergyman himself, Mason was recognized as a successful poet, with one of his volumes, *Spiritual Songs; or, Songs of Praise to Almighty God,* reprinting numerous times. His works, referred to as "free hymns" rather than paraphrases, were a leading influence on the hymns of Isaac Watts. Shortly before Mason's death, he beheld a vision of Christ, and when he spoke of it and preached about it, the entire village (and some neighboring ones as well), gathered in, hunkered down, and waited for Christ's coming. Even after Mason passed away, the eager believers waited for the blessed event.

The use of aromatic resins like frankincense in religious services far predates Christian and Judaic use. Ancient Egyptian carvings depict pharoahs honoring their gods with burning incense, just as contemporary Catholic, Eastern Orthodox, Anglican and Episcopalian, and Lutheran churches do to this day.

As Pants the Hart for Cooling Streams

As the hart panteth after the water brooks, so panteth my soul after thee, O God. — Psalm 42:1

As pants the Hart for cooling Streams
When heated in the chase,
So longs my Soul, O God, for thee
And thy refreshing Grace.

For thee, my God, the living God,
My thirsty Soul doth pine;
O when shall I behold thy Face,
Thou Majesty Divine?

Tears are my constant Food, while thus
Insulting Foes upbraid,
"Deluded Wretch, where's now thy God?
And where his promis'd Aid?"

I sigh when recollecting Thoughts
Those happy Days present,
When I with Troops of pious Friends
Thy temple did frequent.

When I advanced with Songs of Praise,
My solemn Vows to pay,
And led the joyful sacred Throng
That kept the festal day.

One Trouble calls another on,
And bursting o'er my Head,
Fall spouting down, till round my Soul
A roaring Deluge spread.

But when thy Presence, Lord of life,
Has once dispell'd this Storm,
To thee I'll midnight anthems sing,
And midnight Vows perform.

God of my Strength, how long shall I
Like one forgotten mourn?
Forlorn, forsaken, and expos'd
To my Oppressor's Scorn.

Why restless, why cast down, my Soul?
Trust God, and he'll employ
His Aid for thee; convert thy Sighs
To thankful Hymns of Joy.

NAHUM TATE and NICHOLAS BRADY London, England, 1696 *Anglican*
The Roman and Anglican Churches teach that the Bible was divinely inspired, and therefore sacred song should only be a direct or paraphrased version of what was found in Scripture. At the end of the seventeenth century, Irishmen Nahum Tate (England's poet laureate) and Nicholas Brady published *A New Version of the Psalms of David Fitted to the Tunes Used in Churches*, introducing paraphrases of the Psalms that were the next step toward wholly original compositions in English, including this version of Psalm 42. Tate, the son and grandson of clergymen, is famous for his adaptations of Shakespeare and also for the hymn "While Shepherds Watched their Flocks by Night." Nicholas Brady was a vicar, and served as chaplain to King William II and Queen Anne.

LET EVERY HEART PREPARE HIM ROOM
1700–1799

While we sing the Praises of our God in his Church, we are employed in that part of Worship which of all others is the nearest akin to Heaven.... — Isaac Watts

IN THE WINTER OF 1736, John and Charles Wesley, Anglican priests who were en route to the colony of Georgia to serve as missionaries to the Creek Indians, experienced the beginnings of their own conversions instead. A series of storms battered the *Simmonds* as it made its way across the Atlantic. Mountains of water rose up and smashed down from the black night, pouring through the decks as if swallowing the ship whole. The eighty English passengers screamed and wept as the wind slashed through the mainsail. But the twenty-six Moravians on board sang hymns fearlessly in the faith that salvation was theirs, should God call them home that night. John Wesley wrote in his journal of their enviable faith, in comparison to his own "heart of unbelief" and fear of death.

John began learning German on board in an effort to translate their hymns; he compiled and translated enough songs to publish the first hymnal printed in America, *A Collection of Psalms and Hymns,* in 1736. The clarity of the Moravians' faith, paired with their humility, made these ritual-bound priests question their reliance upon good works to save their souls, and led them to trust that Jesus had washed their sins clean. By 1738, both had experienced conversions and began preaching outside established Anglican churches. Back at home in England, along

roadsides, on hilltops, in barns and workshops, thousands gathered to hear them. Charles began writing the hymns that would make him famous, including "Hark, the Herald Angels Sing." Methodism was born.

The quality of church singing at the time left much to be desired. Hymns were sung and psalms were chanted by rote, without feeling and with little grace. Many Christians were upset by this complacency, believing the Word of God should be honored with beauty and fervor. Built upon the works of Paul Gerhardt and Thomas Ken, hymns of an increasingly personal nature were written. Isaac Watts, a Congregational minister, wrote soulful expressions of an individual's commitment to Christ that were also true works of poetry, including "When I Survey the Wondrous Cross." These moving hymns began to reflect a new evangelical form of Christian faith that was spreading across England's towns and cities.

In the colonies, this shift manifested itself in the form of a revival known as the Great Awakening. But in America, the nature of worship revealed a growing sense of independence from European traditions. While most people lived within fifty miles of the Atlantic, brave souls were seeking their fortunes further inland. Settlers carved a living from forests and fields, a process that was lonely, dangerous, and exhausting, but which helped forge the self-determination that has become an American ideal. While these pioneers came from mainstream church backgrounds, their hardscrabble lifestyles didn't lend themselves to long worship services that kept them from the work at hand. Because they were spread out across acres and miles, it was impractical for them to congregate as their parents and grandparents had in towns.

This didn't mean, however, that worship wasn't vitally important. Many received spiritual guidance and nourishment from itinerant preachers who roamed the wilderness and small towns gathering Christians together for prayer meetings. As each new generation came to the fore, fewer and fewer families belonged to specific congregations, and a more individual, less creed-oriented approach to faith became common.

Following the model of the Wesleys and their Oxford University companion, George Whitefield, and his "tongue of fire," this new breed of preachers was emotional and theatrical, delivering heart-stopping messages of salvation through accepting Jesus. They sang hymns of personal experience, like "Amazing Grace," that became rallying cries for Christians—indeed, the men could be heard coming, singing on horseback or atop wagons. Charismatic and filled with a love for God, each man believed that every soul could be saved.

These ministers were among the first to preach to slaves; Whitefield, along with the Quakers, also spoke out against the whole institution of slavery. These men encouraged a direct relationship with God and Jesus, as well as a "social gospel" of Christian responsibility to those in need, and the glory that awaited believers in heaven. Slaves blended these hymns and messages into their own style of worship and music, and spirituals like "City Called Heaven" began to be heard in fields across the South.

Great minds of the Enlightenment, including Isaac Newton, developed observation strategies and analytical systems that changed the very nature of thinking, not just about nature, but also politics, society, and religion—which, more than ever, went heart to head against science. Principles of analysis and scrutiny were also applied to business, driving the Industrial Revolution. Mechanical inventions like the steam engine (which replaced the power of horses for the first time) forever changed commerce and society on both sides of the Atlantic.

Reason, self-reliance, invention, fervor, direct relationships with Higher Powers—all of these elements in their confluence fueled the flames of revolution. The more colonists succeeded on their own, the less they wanted to be told what to do or how to do it by outside forces. By the end of the century, new flags were flying for the United States and France. In the island colony of St. Domingue, the first successful slave rebellion resulted in the overthrow of the French, clearing the way for the first nation led by former slaves—Haiti. Waves of panic rippled across the plantations of the South, but slaves were given even more reason to sing "hallelujah."

There Is a Land of Pure Delight

If the Lord delight in us, then he will bring us into this land, and give it us; a land which floweth with milk and honey.
—Numbers 14:8

There is a Land of pure Delight,
Where Saints Immortal reign;
Infinite Day excludes the Night,
And Pleasures banish Pain.

There everlasting Spring abides,
And never-withering Flowers:
Death like a narrow Sea divides
This heav'nly Land from ours.

Sweet Fields beyond the swelling Flood
Stand dresst in living Green;
So to the Jews Old Canaan stood,
While Jordan roll'd between.

But timorous Mortals start and shrink
To cross this narrow Sea,
And linger shivering on the Brink,
And fear to launch away.

O could we make our Doubts remove,
These gloomy thoughts that rise,
And see the Canaan that we love,
With unbeclouded Eyes.—

Could we but climb where Moses stood,
And view the landscape o'er,
Not Jordan's Stream, nor Death's cold flood
Should fright us from the Shore.

Isaac Watts Southampton, England, 1707 *Congregational*
The year that Watts was born, his father, a minister of the Nonconformist movement, was imprisoned for his belief that the Church of England had not sufficiently distanced itself from the teachings and practices of Rome. After his release he operated a boarding school, and composed sacred verse in his spare time. When Isaac complained about the lifeless singing in churches, his father challenged him to write hymns that would truly inspire congregations. At only twenty years old, Isaac set to the task; in two years he had written the monumental *Hymns and Spiritual Songs,* which included this hymn, titled by him "A Prospect of Heaven Makes Death Easy." The hymnal is an inclusive work, meant for all manner of churches and all levels of education—even the "plainest Souls." But his hymns were not universally embraced at first. Indeed, many scoffed at his work, calling the hymns "Watts's Whims." A student of Hebrew, Greek, and Latin, a poet, and a pastor, Watts wrote hundreds of hymns in addition to other poetic, theological, and scholarly works.

When I Survey the Wondrous Cross

But God forbid that I should glory, save in the cross of our Lord Jesus Christ, by whom the world is crucified unto me, and I unto the world. —Galations 6:14

When I survey the wondrous Cross
Where the young Prince of Glory died,
My richest Gain I count but Loss,
And pour Contempt on all my Pride.

Forbid it, Lord, that I should boast
Save in the Death of Christ my God;
All the vain things that charm me most,
I sacrifice them to his Blood.

See from his Head, his Hands, his Feet,
Sorrow and Love flow mingled down;
Did e'er such Love and Sorrow meet?
Or Thorns compose so rich a Crown?

His dying crimson, like a Robe
Spreads o'er his Body on the Tree,
Then am I dead to all the Globe,
And all the Globe is dead to me.

Were the whole realm of nature mine,
That were a Present far too small;
Love so amazing, so divine
Demands my Soul, my Life, my All.

ISAAC WATTS Southampton, England, 1707 *Congregational*
Watts despaired over the absence of purely Christian thoughts and prayers in the Old Testament Psalms, which were the only sanctioned texts for Calvinist and Anglican as well as Catholic church song. In his hymnal collections, he addressed truly Christian themes like the Crucifixion. He wrote of his mission, "My design was not to exalt myself to the rank and glory of poets, but I was ambitious to be a servant to the churches, and a helper to the joy of the meanest Christian."

This hymn experienced new popularity in the mid-nineteenth century among evangelical groups, who added in a chorus of "Then I'm clinging, clinging, clinging, Oh! I'm clinging to the cross."

Joy to the World

Make a joyful noise unto the Lord, all the earth: make a loud noise, and rejoice, and sing praise. — Psalm 98:4

Joy to the World, the Lord is come;
Let Earth receive her King:
Let every Heart prepare him Room,
And Heaven and Nature sing.

Joy to the Earth, the Savior reigns;
Let Men their Songs employ;
While Fields and Floods, Rocks, Hills and Plains
Repeat the sounding Joy.

No more let Sins and Sorrows grow,
Nor thorns infest the Ground:
He comes to make his Blessings flow
Far as the Curse is found.

He rules the world with Truth and Grace,
And makes the Nations prove
The glories of his Righteousness,
And Wonders of his Love.

Isaac Watts Southampton, England, 1719 *Congregational*
This text is from Watts's second hymnal, *The Psalms of David Imitated in the Language of the New Testament.* It is a liberal paraphrase of Psalm 98, titled "The Messiah's Coming and Kingdom." Set to music, it has become an iconic Christmas carol, although the text makes no explicit reference to Christmas, or even to the birth of Christ. Watts may well have written the hymn on the theme of Christ's second coming, not birth. Included in his many theological writings is *The End of Time,* a book about the Apocalypse. "Let every heart prepare him room," then, is a message to Christians to live in preparation for Christ's return throughout the year.

By the time of this hymnal's publication in 1719, Watts's hymns were fixtures of Congregational services and those of other dissenting sects as well. The new works were even more original, and more emotional, than his previous songs; they made hymn singing an energetic, truly devotional activity that brought great joy to churches in England as well as in the colonies, where Benjamin Franklin published them.

Descend from Heav'n, Immortal Dove

And the Holy Ghost descended in a bodily shape like a dove upon him, and a voice came from heaven, which said, Thou art my beloved Son; in thee I am well pleased. —Luke 3:22

Descend from heav'n, immortal Dove,
Stoop down and take us on thy Wings,
And mount and bear us far above
The reach of these inferior Things:

Beyond, beyond this lower Sky,
Up where eternal Ages roll;
Where solid Pleasures never die,
And Fruits immortal feast the Soul.

O for a Sight, a pleasing Sight
Of our Almighty Father's Throne!
There sits our Savior crowned with Light,
Clothed in a Body like our own.

Adoring Saints around him stand,
And Thrones and Powers before him fall;
The God shines gracious through the Man,
And sheds sweet Glories on them all.

O what amazing Joys they feel
While to their golden Harps they sing,
And sit on every heav'nly Hill,
And spread the Triumphs of their King!

When shall the Day, dear Lord, appear,
That I shall mount to dwell above,
And stand and bow amongst them there,
And view thy Face, and sing, and love?

Isaac Watts Southampton, England, 1719 *Congregational*
Watts was known for the gentle and illustrative nature of his sermons, qualities that are apparent in hymns like this. He was also a highly educated man, studying Hebrew, Latin, and Greek as all classical scholars did (and do) in an effort to read the ancient texts firsthand. His intimate knowledge of the books of the Bible offered him a wide array of themes and motifs that could carry his messages. In New Testament Scripture, the dove symbolizes the Holy Spirit descending after Christ's baptism. It is also a symbol of peace, as in the Old Testament, a dove flies to Noah carrying an olive branch in a symbolic gesture of the end of God's wrath. In early Christian art, the Apostles and saints were represented as doves, symbolizing their roles as representatives of the Holy Ghost.

Who Are These Like Stars Appearing

For the Lamb which is in the midst of the throne shall feed them, and shall lead them unto living fountains of waters:
and God shall wipe away all tears from their eyes. — Revelation 7:17

Who are these, like stars appearing,
These before God's throne who stand?
Each a golden crown is wearing—
Who are all this glorious band?
Alleluia, hark! they sing,
Praising loud their heavenly King.

Who are these, of dazzling brightness,
Cloth'd in God's own righteousness,
These, whose robes of purest whiteness
Shall their lustre still possess,
Still untouch'd by Time's rude hand?
Whence come all this glorious band?

These are they who have contended
For their Saviour's honour long,
Wrestling on till life was ended,
Following not the sinful throng:
These who well the fight sustain'd,
Triumph through the Lamb have gain'd.

These are they whose hearts were riven,
Sore with woe and anguish tried,
Who in prayer full oft have striven
With the God they glorified;
Now their painful conflict o'er,
God has bid them weep no more.

These, like priests, have watched and waited,
Offering up to Christ their will;
Soul and body consecrated,
Day and night to serve Him still:
Now in God's most holy place
Blest they stand before His face.

With that holy throng uniting,
Then what rapture shall be mine!
In the sun's bright beams delighting,
I too like the stars shall shine:
Lord, for this my voice shall raise
Thanks to Thee, and endless praise.

HEINRICH THEOBALD SCHENK Giessen, Germany, 1719 *Lutheran;* translated by Frances Elizabeth Cox, 1841
Schenk, the son of a pastor, was an ordained preacher and professor of classics. He wrote this hymn, "Wer sind
die vor Gottes Throne?" in honor of All Saints Day and All Hallow's Eve—later shortened to Hallowe'en or
Halloween as the previous day has come to be called, which like so many commercial holidays is rooted in a
solemn religious feast day. The holy day honors all the saints, known and unknown. The celebration began as
early as the fourth century; by the eighth century, the date was set as November 1.

In Schenk's Germany, the *Allerheiligen* (All Saints) and *Allerseelen* (All Souls) celebrations and remembrances
were common among both Catholics and Protestants. Not only was this period in November an opportunity to
honor the dead, but it was believed to be a time when the separation between the present and afterworlds was
less pronounced, allowing for visits from spirits. The feast day offered communities the chance to gather and
pray for the dead; the Germans still decorate graves with wreaths and flowers in recognition of the day.

Hark, the Herald Angels Sing

And I will shake all nations, and the desire of all nations shall come: and I will fill this house with glory, saith the Lord of hosts. — Haggai 2:7

Hark, the herald angels sing,
"Glory to the newborn king!"
"Peace on earth and mercy mild,"
"God and sinners reconciled!"

Joyful, all ye nations, rise,
Join the triumph of the skies,
With th' angelic host proclaim,
"Christ is born in Bethlehem!"

Christ by highest heaven adored,
Christ, the everlasting Lord,
Late in time behold him come,
Offspring of a Virgin's womb.

Veiled in flesh, the Godhead see,
Hail the incarnate Deity!
Pleased as man with man to dwell,
Jesus, our Immanuel!

Hail the heavenly Prince of Peace!
Hail the Sun of Righteousness!
Light and life to all he brings,
Risen with healing in his wings.

Mild he lays his glory by,
Born that man no more may die,
Born to raise the sons of earth,
Born to give them second birth.

Come, Desire of nations, come,
Fix in us thy humble home,
Rise, the woman's conquering seed,
Bruise in us the serpent's head.

Now display thy saving power,
Ruined nature now restore,
Now in mystic union join
Thine to ours, and ours to thine.

Adam's likeness, Lord, efface,
Stamp thy image in its place,
Second Adam from above,
Reinstate us in thy love.

Let us thee, though lost, regain,
Thee, the life, the inner Man:
O! to all thyself impart,
Formed in each believing heart.

CHARLES WESLEY London, England, 1739 *Anglican Methodist*

Many hymns, even those by so highly regarded a composer as Reverend Charles Wesley, were rewritten after their original composition to become the lyrics that are now the standard texts. In some instances, just a word or two was replaced; in other cases, whole stanzas were deleted, or entirely new verses by different authors were added in. Such is the case with this famous Christmas carol, which originally began "Hark! How all the welkin rings." *Welkin* is an archaic word meaning "vault of heaven;" Wesley was inspired to write the poem after listening to church bells fill the skies on Christmas Day. (His original manuscript is the frontispiece illustration for this book.) Reverend George Whitefield changed the first words in a 1753 collection—over Wesley's objections, since the account in Luke tells of the angels speaking, not singing—to those we sing today. The song was further amended later in the eighteenth century.

Christmas carols and hymns had been abolished by the English Puritan parliament in 1627 as being part of a "worldly festival"; this was one of the first religious English Christmas carols.

Rise, My Soul, and Stretch Thy Wings

And if thou draw out thy soul to the hungry, and satisfy the afflicted soul; then shall thy light rise in obscurity, and thy darkness be as the noonday… — Isaiah 58:10

Rise, my Soul, and stretch thy Wings,
Thy better Portion trace;
Rise from transitory Things,
Tow'rds Heav'n, thy native Place.
Sun and Moon and Stars decay,
Time shall soon this Earth remove;
Rise, my Soul, and haste away
To seats prepar'd above.

Rivers to the Ocean run,
Nor stay in all their course;
Fire ascending seeks the Sun;
Both speed them to their Source:
So my Soul deriv'd from God,
Pants to view His glorious Face,
Forward tends to His Abode,
To rest in His Embrace.

Fly my Riches, fly my Cares,
Whilst I that Coast explore;
Flatt'ring World, with all thy Snares,
Solicit me no more.
Pilgrims fix not here their Home;
Strangers tarry but a Night,
When the last dear Man is come,
They'll rise to joyous Flight.

Cease, ye Pilgrims, cease to mourn,
Press onward to the Prize;
Soon our Savior will return,
To take thee to the skies:
Yet a Season and you know
Happy Entrance will be giv'n,
All our Sorrows left below,
And earth exchang'd for Heaven.

ROBERT SEAGRAVE Cripplegate, England, 1742 *Anglican Independent*
Seagrave was a Wesleyan disciple famous for his letters, pamphlets, and sermons written for fellow Church of England clergymen, crafted to awaken within them a more fervent commitment to their preaching and good works. Although Anglican, he defended the dissenting Methodists, eventually joining them by preaching as Sunday evening lecturer at Lorimer's Hall, the headquarters church for the guild of spur and bit makers, for whom he wrote this hymn, which he named "The Pilgrim's Song."

One of the most illustrative of sacred songs, Seagrave's work served as a foundation for contemporary hymnist Richard Leach, who likened the soul to song by recasting the lyrics as: "Rise, my song, and stretch thy wings."

Peace Be to This Habitation

Now therefore let it please thee to bless the house of thy servant, that it may be before thee for ever: for thou blessest, O Lord, and it shall be blessed for ever. —1 Chronicles 17:27

Peace be to this Habitation,
Peace on All that here reside!
Let the Unknown Peace of God
With the Man of Peace abide!
Let the Spirit now come down,
Let the Blessing now take place!
Son of peace, receive thy Crown,
Fullness of the Gospel Grace.

Christ, my Master, and my Lord,
Let me Thy Forerunner be,
O be mindful of Thy Word,
Visit them, and visit me:
To this House, and All herein,
Now let Thy Salvation come,
Save our Souls from Inbred Sin,
Make them Thine Eternal Home.

Let us never, never rest
Till the Promise is fulfill'd,
Till we are of Thee possest,
Wash'd, and sanctified, and seal'd:
Till we all in Love renew'd,
Find that Pearl that Adam lost,
Temples of the Living God.
Father, Son, and Holy Ghost.

CHARLES WESLEY London, England, 1742 *Anglican Methodist*
John Wesley, in his *Sermons on Several Occasions,* included a sermon by his brother Charles that was delivered to the University of Oxford in 1742. In its text, Charles speaks of the need for Christians to be "an habitation of God through his Spirit; and, through his Spirit dwelling in us, to be saints here, and partakers of the inheritance of the saints in light." Charles called this hymn "The Salutation."

Charles's own home was a blessed one. From his journals and letters, it's clear that his marriage to Sally Gwynne, the year this hymn was published, made him the happiest of men. She often accompanied him on his ministerial rounds, and shared his love of music. Of his missionary work she once wrote to him "My prayers were almost swallowed up in Praises for the unspeakable Blessings the Lord had made me a partaker of, thro' Your Ministry...."

See How Great a Flame Aspires

For the law was given by Moses, but grace and truth came by Jesus Christ. —John 1:17

See how great a Flame aspires,
Kindled by a Spark of Grace!
Jesu's Love the Nations fires,
Sets the Kingdoms on a Blaze.
To bring Fire on Earth He came;
Kindled in some Hearts it is:
O that All might catch the Flame,
All partake the Glorious Bliss!

When He first the Work begun,
Small and feeble was his Day:
Now the Word doth swiftly run;
Now it wins its widening Way,
More and more it spreads, and grows
Ever mighty to prevail,
Sin's strong holds it now o'erthrows—
Shakes the trembling Gates of Hell.

Sons of God, your Saviour praise,
He the Door hath open'd wide,
He hath given the Word of Grace,
Jesu's Word is glorified:
Jesus, mighty to redeem,
He alone the Work hath wrought;
Worthy is the Work of Him,
Him who spake a world from Nought.

Saw ye not the Cloud arise,
Little as a Human Hand?
Now it spreads along the Skies,
Hangs o'er all the thirsty land!
Lo! the Promise of a Shower
Drops already from above
But the Lord shall shortly pour
All the Spirit of his Love.

CHARLES WESLEY Newcastle, England, 1749 *Methodist*

John and Charles Wesley took the Gospel to towns and cities across England, Scotland, Wales, and Ireland. They were welcomed with open arms—at least by the poor and working classes. One of the communities they visited was Newcastle, where coal miners, or colliers as they were known, were an especially enthusiastic group. Charles, the "Poet of Methodism," wrote this hymn—one of thousands penned during his lifetime—as a testament to the brothers' successful ministry there. He may have been inspired by watching the fires that burned to make charcoal, which were said to light the night skies as bright as day. John was fully supportive of his brother's poetic works, believing that hymns need be of the highest literary merit, "such as would sooner provoke a critic to turn Christian than a Christian to turn critic."

I Want a Principle Within

And Moses said unto the people, Fear not: for God is come to prove you, and that his fear may be before your faces, that ye sin not. Exodus 20:20

Almighty God of Truth and Love,
In me thy Power impart;
The Mountain from my Soul remove,
The Hardness from my Heart.
My most obdurate Heart subdue,
In honour of Thy Son,
And now the gracious Wonder show,
And take away the Stone.

I want a Principle within,
Of jealous, godly fear,
A Sensibility of Sin,
A Pain to feel it near:
I want the first Approach to feel
Of Pride, or fond Desire,
To catch the Wandrings of my Will,
And quench the kindling Fire.

From Thee that I no more may part,
No more Thy Goodness grieve,
The filial Awe, the fleshly Heart,
The tender Conscience give.
Quick as the Apple of an Eye,
O God, my Conscience make;
Awake my Soul when Sin is nigh,
And keep it still awake.

O may the least Omission pain
My well-instructed Soul,
And drive me to the Blood again,
Which makes the Wounded whole:
More of this tender Spirit, more
Of this Affliction send,
And spread the *Moral Sense* all o'er,
'Till Pain with Life shall end.

CHARLES WESLEY London, England, 1749 *Anglican Methodist*
John and Charles Wesley lived in an era of intellectual enlightenment, but also physical suffering and poverty. In the London of their time, adults and children could be legally hanged for more than one hundred different offenses, including petty theft. The child mortality rate was staggering. Alcohol abuse was a pervasive social disease. The brothers believed that leading people to God, to the salvation promised through Jesus' death, would bring changes in society at large as well as in individual souls. They preached that charitable works and donations to the poor were a core concern of their fellowship. Conversion by conversion, their Methodists did effect change, in the prison system, in education, and in health concerns, joining their efforts with the good works of the Jews, Roman Catholics, and other dissenters like the Quakers. Charles called this "For a Tender Conscience."

Come, Thou Fount of Every Blessing

And all these blessings shall come on thee, and overtake thee, if thou shalt hearken unto the voice of the Lord thy God.
—Deuteronomy 28:2

Come, thou Fount of every blessing,
Tune my heart to sing thy grace;
Streams of mercy never ceasing,
Call for songs of loudest praise.
Teach me some melodious sonnet,
Sung by flaming tongues above.
Praise the mount! I'm fixt upon it,
Mount of God's unchanging love.

Here I raise my Ebenezer;
Hither by the grace I've come;
So I hope by Thy good pleasure,
Shortly to arrive at home.
Jesus sought me when a stranger,
Wand'ring from the fold of God;
He, to rescue me from danger,
Interpos'd with precious blood.

O! to grace how great a debtor
Daily I'm constrain'd to be;
Let thy grace, now like a fetter,
Bind my wand'ring heart to thee;
Prone to wander, Lord, I feel it,
Prone to leave the God I love;
Take my heart, O take and seal it,
Seal it from thy courts above.

O that day when freed from sinning,
I shall see thy lovely face;
Cloth'd then in blood-washed linen,
How I'll sing thy sov'reign grace:
Come, my Lord, no longer tarry,
Take my ransom'd soul away;
Send thine angels now to carry
Me to realms of endless day.

ROBERT ROBINSON London, England, 1758 *Baptist*
While still a teenager, Robinson was sent to apprentice with a barber in London, but was said to have fallen in with a rough crowd. His "gang" attended a Methodist service with the intention of hassling the preacher and congregants, but the sermon by Great Awakening reverend George Whitefield on Matthew 3:7 changed Robinson, who promptly underwent a conversion. Within three years he began to preach as well, and to convert others, at first as a Methodist and later as a Baptist. Toward the end of his life, after a successful career as a pastor in Cambridge, Robinson's beliefs shifted again toward more intellectual Unitarianism.

   The Ebenezer was the stone raised by Samuel ("heard of God") as a monument to God's aid during a decisive battle against the Philistines. Soon after this hymn was written, the American Colonial and French "Samuels" would lead their people and rise against their own oppressors to win independence.

Thou Lovely Source of True Delight

Let thy tender mercies come unto me, that I may live: for thy law is my delight. — Psalm 119:77

Thou lovely source of true delight,
Whom I unseen adore;
Unveil Thy beauties to my sight,
That I may love thee more.

Thy glory o'er creation shines;
But in thy sacred word,
I read in fairer, brighter lines,
My bleeding, dying Lord.

'Tis here, whene'er my comforts droop,
And sins and sorrows rise,
Thy love with cheerful beams of hope,
My fainting heart supplies.

But ah, too soon, the pleasing scene
Is clouded o'er with pain;
My gloomy fears rise dark between,
And I again complain.

Jesus, my Lord, my life, my light,
O come with blissful ray;
Break radiant through the shades of night,
And chase my fears away.

Then shall my soul with rapture trace
The wonders of thy love;
But the full glories of Thy face
Are only known above.

ANNE STEELE Broughton, England, 1760 *Baptist*
Steele was the eldest daughter of a timber merchant who also served as an unsalaried Baptist preacher. She led what could have seemed a cursed life to some: her mother died when she was three, she suffered an injury that made her a lifelong invalid at nineteen, and when she was twenty-one, the man she was being courted by drowned. Yet somehow, her absolute faith in God's sovereignty—and a marked sense of humor—helped carry her. Writing under the nom de plume Theodosia, and while aiding her father with his pastoral duties, she wrote three volumes of poetry, the proceeds of which she donated to charity. She also wrote 144 hymns for her parish's use, becoming the first English-speaking female poet whose work appeared in established hymnals. She was known for her intense personal devotion and evangelic fervor. She led a rich life of creative work, church service, and fruitful friendships with many other authors, in spite of her confinement. Her epitaph reads: "Silent the lyre, and dumb the tuneful tongue / That sung on earth her great Redeemer's praise; / But now in heaven she joins the angelic song / In more harmonious, more exalted lays."

Amazing Grace

*And I thank Christ Jesus our Lord, who hath enabled me, for that he counted me faithful, putting me into the ministry;
Who was before a blasphemer, and a persecutor, and injurious: but I obtained mercy, because I did it ignorantly in unbelief.*
—1 Timothy 1:12-13

Amazing grace! (how sweet the sound)
That sav'd a wretch like me!
I once was lost, but now am found,
Was blind, but now I see.

'Twas grace that taught my heart to fear,
And grace my fears reliev'd;
How precious did that grace appear
The hour I first believ'd!

Thro' many dangers, toils and snares,
I have already come;
'Tis grace has brought me safe thus far,
And grace will lead me home.

The Lord has promis'd good to me,
His Word my hope secures;
He will my Shield and Portion be,
As long as life endures.

Yea, when this flesh and heart shall fail,
And mortal life shall cease,
I shall possess, within the vail,
A life of joy and peace.

The earth shall soon dissolve like snow,
The sun forbear to shine;
But God, Who call'd me here below,
Will be forever mine.

JOHN NEWTON Olney, England, 1773 *Anglican Independent*

"John Newton. Clerk, once an Infidel and Libertine, a Servant of Slaves in Africa, was Preserved, Restored, Pardoned, and Appointed to Preach the Faith he had so long laboured to destroy." So reads Newton's self-composed epitaph, proclaiming his journey from an early life as a slave ship captain through the conversion that led him to write the most popular English hymn of all time.

Newton, like so many children of those times, lost his mother at a tender age and was sent away to boarding schools. He was full of energy and had a thirst for adventure, leaving school at eleven to begin his career as a seaman. The life of a Royal Navy sailor was colored by unsavory characters and practices, the most unholy of which at this time was the capture and sale of Africans as slaves.

Newton eventually became captain of his own slave ship. On a stormy trip in his early twenties, however, when the ship might have been wrecked, Newton—in between manning the pumps and steering the wheel—read medieval monk Thomas à Kempis's book *Imitation of Christ*. Between the fear for his life and ship, and the apparent doubts about his moral choices that surfaced as he read, Newton began to be reformed, and reborn. Although he didn't abandon the slave trade immediately, it wasn't long before he spoke out against it and took steps toward preaching. While serving as the vicar of Olney he wrote the poem "Faith's Review and Expectation" as a hymn for his 1773 New Year's Morning sermon. It later became known as "Amazing Grace," set to the old American plantation tune "Loving Lambs." Although influenced by the Wesleys and other Evangelical leaders, Newton stayed within the Church of England, stepping outside of its traditions only by ministering in old barns and abandoned buildings in addition to his church—and by singing hymns.

Sometimes a Light Surprises

Therefore the redeemed of the Lord shall return, and come with singing unto Zion; and everlasting joy shall be upon their head: they shall obtain gladness and joy; and sorrow and mourning shall flee away. — Isaiah 51:11

Sometimes a light surprises
The Christian while he sings;
It is the Lord, Who rises
With healing in His wings:
When comforts are declining,
He grants the soul again
A season of clear shining,
To cheer it after rain.

In holy contemplation
We sweetly then pursue
The theme of God's salvation,
And find it ever new.
Set free from present sorrow,
We cheerfully can say,
Let the unknown tomorrow
Bring with it what it may.

It can bring with it nothing
But He will bear us through;
Who gives the lilies clothing
Will clothe His people, too;
Beneath the spreading heavens,
No creature but is fed;
And He Who feeds the ravens
Will give His children bread.

Though vine nor fig tree neither
Their wonted fruit should bear,
Though all the field should wither,
Nor flocks nor herds be there;
Yet God the same abiding,
His praise shall tune my voice,
For while in Him confiding,
I cannot but rejoice.

WILLIAM COWPER Olney, England, 1779 *Anglican Independent*
A debilitating depression plagued Cowper his entire life, forcing a stay in an asylum at one point, and leading him to contemplate suicide by a series of means, none of which he could succumb to. He credited the powers of divine intervention for foiling his dark plans. His famous hymn "There Is a Fountain Filled with Blood" (called the "battle hymn" of Evangelicals in the mid-nineteenth century) was written soon after that dark time in his life. Cowper eventually moved to Olney, to a home neighboring John Newton's vicarage. The country setting helped to some degree; Cowper took up gardening, kept rabbits, and aided Newton with the sick of the parish. The two men were close, but Newton struggled to keep Cowper above his melancholy. Partly as a means of distraction, Newton suggested that they work together on a hymnal. *Olney Hymns* was published in 1779 with hundreds of works by Newton, including "Amazing Grace," and many by Cowper.

This hymn, with its hope-filled words, shows a lighter side of Cowper's nature and is a testament to the power of song. Cowper called it "Joy and Peace in Believing."

God Moves in a Mysterious Way

That their hearts might be comforted, being knit together in love, and unto all riches of the full assurance of understanding, to the acknowledgement of the mystery of God, and of the Father, and of Christ; In whom are hid all the treasures of wisdom and knowledge. —Colossians 2:2-3

God moves in a mysterious way
His wonders to perform;
He plants His footsteps in the sea,
And rides upon the storm.

Deep in unfathomable mines
Of never-failing skill
He treasures up His bright designs
And works His sovereign will.

Ye fearful saints, fresh courage take;
The clouds ye so much dread
Are big with mercy, and shall break
In blessings on your head.

Judge not the Lord by feeble sense,
But trust Him for His grace:
Behind a frowning providence
He hides a smiling face.

His purposes will ripen fast,
Unfolding every hour;
The bud may have a bitter taste,
But sweet will be the flower.

Blind unbelief is sure to err,
And scan His work in vain;
God is His own Interpreter
And He will make it plain.

WILLIAM COWPER Olney, England, 1779 *Anglican Independent*
Olney Hymns proved to be an illustrious literary beginning for Cowper, who continued to write hymns and other poems (one of which was devoted to the antislavery effort) throughout his life. He became a founding member of the English romantic movement, with its emphasis on the pleasures of nature and everyday scenes.

Cowper titled this hymn "Light Shining out of Darkness"—a theme that was the leitmotif of his life, both in his struggles with depression and his compromised eyesight.

Precious Bible! What a Treasure

For the word of God is quick, and powerful, and sharper than any twoedged sword, piercing even to the dividing asunder of soul and spirit, and of the joints and marrow, and is a discerner of the thoughts and intents of the heart. —Hebrews 4:12

Precious Bible! what a treasure
Does the Word of God afford!
All I want for life or pleasure,
Food and med'cine, shield and sword:
Let the world account me poor,
Having this I need no more.

Food to which the world's a stranger,
Here my hungry soul enjoys;
Of excess there is no danger,
Though it fills, it never cloys:
On a dying Christ I feed,
He is meat and drink indeed.

When my faith is faint and sickly,
Or when Satan wounds my mind,
Cordials to revive me quickly,
Healing med'cines here I find:
To the promises I flee,
Each affords a remedy.

In the hour of dark temptation
Satan cannot make me yield;
For the Word of consolation
Is to me a mighty shield
While the scripture truths are sure,
From his malice I'm secure.

Vain his threats to overcome me,
When I take the Spirits' sword;
Then with ease I drive him from me.
Satan trembles at the Word:
'Tis a sword for conquest made,
Keen the edge, and strong the blade.

Shall I envy then the miser
Doting on his golden store?
Sure I am, or should be wiser,
I am rich, 'tis he is poor:
Jesus gives me in his Word,
Food and med'cine, shield and sword.

John Newton Olney, England, 1779 *Anglican Independent*
Newton was fortunate to have been born at a time when there were copies of the Bible readily available to be read and shared in his native tongue. It had been a long time coming. English translations of the Bible began as early as 1382 with John Wycliffe's handwritten version. He and others including William Tyndale were martyred for their efforts in bringing the Word to the people, which was considered, at the time, to be blasphemous in anything but Latin or the original Hebrew and Greek. However, following Henry VIII's split from Rome and founding of the Church of England, there were so many translations that King James called for one definitive version to be drafted. The King James Bible was published in 1611; this was still the standard edition in 1779 and continues to be widely used because of the great beauty of its language. Today, the Bible is printed in more than one thousand languages, following the trails of missionaries who have traveled the globe.

Tho' Troubles Assail

The Spirit itself beareth witness with our spirit, that we are the children of God: And if children, then heirs; heirs of God, and joint-heirs with Christ; if so be that we suffer with him, that we may be also glorified together. For I reckon that the sufferings of this present time are not worthy to be compared with the glory which shall be revealed in us. —Romans 8:16–18

Tho' troubles assail
And dangers affright,
Tho' friends should all fail
And foes all unite;
Yet one thing secures us,
Whatever betide,
The promise assures us,
'The Lord will provide.'

The birds, without barn
And storehouse, are fed,
From them let us learn
To trust for our bread.
His saints, what is fitting,
Shall ne'er be denied
So long as 'tis written,
'The Lord will provide.'

We may, like the ships,
By tempests be tossed,
Or perilous deeps,
But cannot be lost:
Though Satan enrages
The wind and the tide,
The promise engages,
'The Lord will provide.'

When Satan appears
To stop up our path,
And fill us with fears,
We triumph by faith.
He cannot take from us,
Tho' oft he has try'd,
This heart cheering promise,
'The Lord will provide.'

No strength of our own
Or goodness we claim;
Yet since we have known
The Savior's great name,
In this our strong tower
For safety we hide,
The Lord is our power,
'The Lord will provide.'

When life sinks apace,
And death is in view,
The word of his grace
Shall comfort us through:
No fearing, nor doubting,
With Christ on our side,
We hope to die shouting,
'The Lord will provide.'

JOHN NEWTON Olney, England, 1779 *Anglican Independent*
When Newton and his wife, Mary, settled in the lace-making village of Olney in 1764, they found the town in dire need of uplifting. Dirty and poor, Olney residents were described by William Cowper as "half starved and ragged." The two men joined forces, distributing funds to the needy from Newton's annuity and offering comfort to the sick and dying in addition to feeding their souls with intelligent and charismatic sermons—and some of the most moving hymns ever written.

Blest Be the Tie That Binds

And he answering said, Thou shalt love the Lord thy God with all thy heart, and with all thy soul, and with all thy strength, and with all thy mind; and thy neighbour as thyself. —Luke 10:27

Blest be the tie that binds
Our hearts in Christian love;
The fellowship of kindred minds
Is like to that above.

Before our Father's throne
We pour our ardent prayers;
Our fears, our hopes, our aims are one
Our comforts and our cares.

We share our mutual woes,
Our mutual burdens bear;
And often for each other flows
The sympathizing tear.

When we asunder part,
It gives us inward pain;
But we shall still be join'd
And hope to meet again.

This glorious hope revives
Our courage by the way;
While each in expectation lives,
And longs to see the day.

From sorrow, toil and pain,
And sin, we shall be free,
And perfect love and friendship reign
Thro' all eternity.

JOHN FAWCETT Wainsgate, England, 1782 *Baptist*

The story behind Fawcett's hymn is one of the love that develops between a pastor and a congregation. Born in poverty in Yorkshire, England, Fawcett was converted at sixteen after hearing George Whitefield preach and ten years later was a Baptist minister himself. He was sent to the small town of Wainsgate in northern England, where he struggled to build his ministry and his family from a modest salary. He was later offered the opportunity to move to London to a more prestigious and lucrative position, which he accepted. With trunks packed and wagons ready to head south, the Fawcetts said their goodbyes surrounded by their tearful parishioners. John and his wife couldn't bear the pain of separation, so the wagons and trunks were soon unpacked. Fawcett is believed to have written this poem, first entitled "Brotherly Love," in honor of this experience; it is often sung as a farewell hymn today.

City Called Heaven

And he carried me away in the spirit to a great and high mountain, and shewed me that great city, the holy Jerusalem, descending out of heaven from God. — Revelation 21:10

I am a poor pilgrim of sorrow
I'm tossed in this wide world alone
No hope have I for tomorrow
I'm trying to make heav'n my home.

Sometimes I am tossed and driven, Lord,
Sometimes I don't know where to roam,
I've heard of a city called Heaven
I've started to make it my home.

My mother reached that pure glory
My father's still walkin' in sin
My brothers and sisters won't own me
Because I'm tryin' to get in.

Sometimes I am tossed and driven, Lord,
Sometimes I don't know where to roam,
I've heard of a city called Heaven
I've started to make it my home.

I know dark clouds will gather 'round me,
I know my way is rough and steep,
Yet bright fields lie just before me,
Where God's redeemed their vigils keep.

Sometimes I am tossed and driven, Lord,
Sometimes I don't know where to roam,
I've heard of a city called Heaven
I've started to make it my home.

TRADITIONAL SPIRITUAL

Slaves, when they were offered spiritual guidance and instruction at all, were taught that their reward would be in heaven—that only their souls were free here on earth, not their bodies. Their songs naturally reinforced this promise of release from the horrors of enslavement. In Revelation, the city of heaven is described in opulent, elegant terms, promising twelve pearl gates within walls of jasper, sapphire, emerald, and other precious stones, surrounding a city made of pure gold. Imagining a place of such great beauty, where God would wipe all tears from their eyes and take away their pain and sorrow, would have been uplifting indeed in the face of the daily indignations and backbreaking work they endured. Heaven, within the text of a spiritual, referred not only to the afterlife, but to a better place and freer circumstance on this earth, as well as the "Kingdom of Heaven" within.

'TIS THE GIFT TO BE FREE
1800–1899

It is so sweet to look up to Jesus, in the joy of His keeping, and to tell Him how one longs, not merely not to grieve Him any more, but to please, really and truly please *Him, all the days of my life.* —Frances Ridley Havergal

IN AUGUST OF 1801, twenty thousand men, women, and children from the Bourbon County hills surrounding Cane Ridge, Kentucky, traveled on foot, on horseback, and by wagon to a four-day spiritual revival. Their common hope was the "blessed assurance" of salvation, of having their sins washed away by Christ's sacrifice for them. They hewed rough pews from blue ash logs. They testified from tree stumps. Lanterns hanging in oak and chestnut trees shed their light on hour upon hour of hymn singing, shouting, and praying. Ministers demanded repentance from timber platforms that rose high above the cane fields and forests. People fell to the ground in droves, shaking and weeping through their conversions. One eyewitness wrote, "The noise was like the roar of Niagara. At one time I saw at least five hundred swept down in a moment as if a battery of a thousand guns had been opened upon them, and then immediately followed shrieks and shouts that rent the very heavens."

Revivals had been features of outlying territories since the early days of itinerant preachers like the Wesley brothers and George Whitefield, but nothing on the scale of this epic "camp meeting" had ever occurred; its unprecedented, fortuitous success became the gold standard for all other evangelical gatherings, with every preacher hoping he could lead so many to save their own souls. Freedom came from free will, and salvation was guaranteed for anyone who actively accepted Jesus as their Savior. While the Baptists and Methodists simultaneously grew their ranks by millions, and mainstream churches dismissed the events as fanaticism, Cane Ridge inspired a movement that broke the bounds of traditional denominations—an all-embracing Christian melting pot. The spirit of these meetings was a manifestation of the broader American insistence on autonomy, freedom, and, increasingly, equality. Anyone, black or white, could preach. Rich and poor worshiped side by side. All were free in their love of Christ, who was now seen as a constant presence in one's life, not a distant deity—a shift that inspired hymns like Joseph Scriven's "What a Friend We Have in Jesus."

Nineteenth-century America took freedom as its theme. The nation expanded following the explorations of Lewis and Clark and the rail lines laid for the newly-invented steam train. Individuals were free to succeed on their own terms, by cutting Conestoga wagon trails into the prairie, sweating in factories, or setting out for the gold rush. Immigrants from Europe and Asia were free to leave behind the restrictions of the Old Countries and build a dynamic new society. Workers were free to form unions and go on strike to reduce the hours in the work day and demand safety measures. Scientists were free to push the boundaries of knowledge. Slaves were free to sing "Go Down, Moses," though their backs were bent in unpaid labor and their families were torn apart.

Some freedoms came at great cost, many of which were rooted in the expansionist creed of Manifest Destiny, the belief that Americans had a God-given right to take as much land as they could muster the strength to claim. In addition to the Lewis and Clark expedition, President Jefferson's acquisition of the Louisiana Territory from France in 1803 encouraged Americans to push west, with or without formal treaties granting them permission to do so. California, Oregon, and Texas became American soil only after bloody conflicts with Mexico. Parts of Georgia and Florida were cleared for settlers by evicting Native American tribes like the Cherokee, forcing a thousand-mile march to the Oklahoma reservations along which thousands died. Freedoms of industry and enterprise left slums and hazardous conditions for workers in their wake. And the fight for the abolition of slavery, begun in the eighteenth century, and which had succeeded in England in 1833, would go head to head against the freedom of states' rights, dividing the nation and leaving more than a million casualties from coast to coast.

In reaction to society's ills and tragedies, a number of religiously based relief groups were founded. While missionary work continued in the distant outposts of the empires, the focus began to shift to caring for those at home as well. In response to the slum conditions and overcrowded prisons that sprang up in tandem with the Industrial Revolution, the Young Men's Christian Association (YMCA), a Bible study and prayer group founded by nonsectarian evangelicals, was founded in London in 1844. The movement came to North America by 1851; during the Civil War—an era before the establishment of the Red Cross—volunteers like Walt Whitman lent comfort to troops on both sides. By 1866, the mission expanded its course to "the improvement of the spiritual, mental, social, and physical condition of young men," an early form of the mind-body-spirit ethic that pervades the healing industry today. The Salvation Army was founded in 1865 by William Booth, a London minister whose compelling sermons inspired action. This new breed of missionary preached in Sunday schools, on street corners, and in saloons, in an effort to free children from disease, women from destitution, men from addiction, and everyone from eternal damnation.

Through all of these movements toward freedom, women became bona fide members of the workforce, relief efforts, and artistic community. From Phoebe Hinsdale Brown's writing while balancing a baby on one knee to Katharine Lee Bates's climbing Pike's Peak and becoming inspired to write "America the Beautiful," women made the world hear their voices.

When Spring Unlocks the Flowers

For, lo, the winter is past, the rain is over and gone; The flowers appear on the earth; the time of the singing of birds is come.
—Song of Solomon 2:11–12

When spring unlocks the flowers
To paint the laughing soil;
When summer's balmy breezes
Refresh the mower's toil;
When winter holds in frosty chains
The fallow and the flood;
In God the earth rejoiceth still
And owns her Maker good.

The birds that wake the morning
And those that love the shade;
The winds that sweep the ocean,
Or lull the drowsy glade;
The sun that from his amber bower
Rejoices on his way,
The moon and stars, their Ruler's state
In silent pomp display.

Shall man the heir of nature,
Expectant of the sky—
Shall man alone, unthankful,
The little praise deny?
No, let the sun forsake his course,
The seasons cease to be—
Thee, Maker, shall we yet adore,
And Saviour, honour Thee.

The flowers of spring may wither,
The fruits of summer fade,
The winter fall untimely,
The birds forsake the shade,
The rivers fail, the ocean's tide
Unlearn his old decree,
But Lord, in nature's dying hour,
Our love shall cling to Thee.

REGINALD HEBER Hodnet, England, 1816 *Anglican*

By the age of five, Heber had memorized the Bible so thoroughly that he could cite chapter and verse of any given quotation. His early schooling in the language and stories of the Bible served him well, as did his education at All Souls College, Oxford, as he went on to become one of hymnody's most famous and beloved poets. He served as rector for Hodnet before being named bishop of Calcutta. In India, he was known for traveling great distances that his fellow Englishmen dared not attempt in order to serve his diocese, which at that time included all of Australia and Ceylon (present-day Sri Lanka). He ordained Indians, was sensitive to their culture, and learned their languages to preach directly to the growing flock—all in the three years before his premature death.

One of the many quotes that survive Heber is this from his last sermon before his departure for India: "According to the gospels there are only two kinds of human beings; those we love and those we ought to love." His words, from sermons, secular poems, and hymns, are memorable for their beauty and messages. In previous centuries, the first stanza of this hymn served not only for holy purposes, but also as an inspirational quote for samplers; the words are often found in quotation collections even today.

I Love to Steal Awhile Away

Many sorrows shall be to the wicked: but he that trusteth in the Lord, mercy shall compass him about. —Psalm 32:10

Yes, when the toilsome day is gone,
And night with banners gray,
Steals silently the glade along
In twilight's soft array,

I love to steal awhile away
From little ones and care,
And spend the hours of setting day
In gratitude and prayer.

I love to feast on Nature's scenes
When falls the evening dew,
And dwell upon her silent themes,
Forever rich and new.

I love in solitude to shed
The penitential tear,
And all God's promises to plead
Where none can see or hear.

I love to think on mercies past,
And future good implore,
And all my cares and sorrows cast
On him whom I adore.

I love to meditate on death!
When shall his message come,
With friendly smiles to steal my breath,
And take an exile home?

I love by faith to take a view
Of brighter scenes in Heaven:
Thy sight doth all my strength renew,
While here by storms I'm driven.

Thus, when life's toilsome day is o'er,
May its departing ray,
Be calm as this impressive hour,
And lead to endless day.

PHOEBE HINSDALE BROWN Ellington, Connecticut, 1818 *Congregational*
Unlike so many hymnists who were born to prominent families and material comfort, Brown lived a life of deprivation, drudgery, and menial labor. Orphaned at the age of two, she was left to cruel relatives who kept a county jail. Later, as a mother, wife, and caretaker of an invalid sister, Brown had little time to herself. She wrote that she craved a room of her own, but in her crowded home and life, privacy and free time were not luxuries she regularly enjoyed. Instead she "stole away" in the evenings, strolling toward a wealthy neighbor's fragrant elm-lined garden, where she was allowed an "uninterrupted communion with God." The haughty lady of the manor, however, had noticed her, and asked why she was milling about the property without making herself known. Horrified, Brown sat down that evening with a baby on her lap and penned what she originally called "My Apology for My Twilight Rambles, Addressed to a Lady." The poem "A Twilight Hymn" was first published in *Village Hymns for Social Worship* in 1824. The men who edited the book, however, took it upon themselves to rewrite Brown's words and eliminate four stanzas altogether. This was a common practice, but in this case Brown's meaning was altered to soften the sense of burden she had conveyed, which may have sounded unseemly for a wife and mother of that time. The words above are Brown's original version, the beauty of which is even more remarkable in the knowledge that the author had only three months of formal education. In addition to her legacy as a hymnist, one of Brown's "little ones" became the first Christian missionary to Japan, Reverend S. R. Brown.

Lord, Teach Us How to Pray Aright

And it came to pass, that, as he was praying in a certain place, when he ceased, one of his disciples said unto him, Lord, teach us to pray, as John also taught his disciples. —Luke 11:1–4

Lord, teach us how to pray aright,
With reverence and with fear;
Though dust and ashes in thy sight,
We may, we must draw near.

We perish if we cease from prayer;
O grant us power to pray;
And when to meet thee we prepare,
Lord, meet us by the way.

Burden'd with guilt, convinced of sin,
In weakness, want, and woe,
Fighting without, and fears within,
Lord, whither shall we go?

Faith in the only sacrifice
That can for sin atone;
To cast our hopes, to fix our eyes,
On Christ, on Christ alone.

Give deep humility;—the sense
Of godly sorrow give;
A strong desiring confidence
To see thy face and live;—

Patience to watch, and wait, and weep,
Though mercy long delay;
Courage our fainting souls to keep,
And trust thee though thou slay.

Give these, and then thy will be done,
Thus strengthened with all might,
We, by thy Spirit and through thy Son,
Shall pray, and pray aright.

JAMES MONTGOMERY Sheffield, England, 1818 *Moravian*
Montgomery's father was a Moravian minister; both parents served as missionaries to Barbados in the late eighteenth century, dying within a year of each other while he was still a boy. His life quickly turned from one of religious observance to one of worldly pleasure as he was shuffled from home to home. He soon ran away, with just pennies and poems in his pocket. He found odd jobs with a baker and a grocer before landing a post with a publisher and bookseller, which both offered him exposure to literary minds and opened publishing opportunities to him. Montgomery was in the end an editor and newspaper publisher by trade. His editorial decisions earned him two stays in prison, once as punishment for publishing a poem that glorified the fall of the Bastille in Revolutionary France, and again for critically reporting on a military response to a riot. His social conscience led him to help with foreign missions as well as local philanthropic efforts with young chimney sweeps. John Julian, the eminent nineteenth-century hymn scholar, described Montgomery's work as "richly poetic without exuberance, dogmatic without uncharitableness, tender without sentimentality." The esteemed twentieth-century hymnologist Erik Routley called Montgomery "without any question, on the verdict of posterity, the greatest of Christian lay hymn writers."

Angels from the Realms of Glory

That at the name of Jesus every knee should bow, of things in heaven, and things in earth, and things under the earth;
And that every tongue should confess that Jesus Christ is Lord, to the glory of God the Father. —Philippians 2:10–11

Angels, from the realms of glory,
Wing your flight o'er all the earth;
Ye, who sang creation's story
Now proclaim Messiah's birth.
Come and worship,
Worship Christ, the newborn King.

Shepherds, in the field abiding,
Watching o'er your flock by night,
God with us is now residing;
Yonder shines the infant light:
Come and worship,
Worship Christ, the newborn King.

Sages, leave your contemplations,
Brighter visions beam afar;
God with man is now residing;
Ye have seen his natal star.
Come and worship,
Worship Christ, the newborn King.

Saints, before the altar bending,
Watching long with hope and fear,
Suddenly the Lord descending,
In his temple shall appear;
Come and worship,
Worship Christ, the newborn King.

Sinners, wrung with true repentance,
Doom'd for guilt to endless pains,
Justice now repeals the sentence,
Mercy calls you,—break your chains:
Come and worship
Worship Christ, the newborn King.

JAMES MONTGOMERY Fulneck, England, 1819 *Moravian*
Montgomery was the owner and publisher of the *Sheffield Iris* in addition to his work as an author and political activist. He published numerous volumes of poetry and wrote hundreds of hymns, honoring the heritage of singing that was so integral a part of worship for the Moravians. Before Christmas one year, in his last-minute search for material for the Christmas Eve edition of his paper, he read through the scriptural accounts of the birth of Jesus and took time away from his daily duties to pen this famous carol.

Lord, With Glowing Heart I'd Praise Thee

For by grace are ye saved through faith; and that not of yourselves: it is the gift of God. —Ephesians 2:8

Lord, with glowing heart I'd praise Thee,
For the bliss Thy love bestows,
For the pard'ning grace that saves me,
And the peace that from it flows:
Help, O God, my weak endeavor;
This dull soul to rapture raise:
Thou must light the flame, or never
Can my love be warm'd to praise.

Praise, my soul, the God that sought thee,
Wretched wand'rer, far astray;
Found thee lost, and kindly brought thee
From the paths of death away;
Praise, with love's devoutest feeling,
Him who saw thy guilt-born fear,
And the light of hope revealing,
Bade the blood-stain'd cross appear.

Praise thy Savior God that drew thee
To that cross, new life to give,
Held a blood-seal'd pardon to Thee,
Bade thee look to him and live.
Praise, the grace whose threats alarm'd thee,
Rous'd thee from thy fatal ease;
Praise the grace whose promise warm'd thee,
Praise the grace that whisper'd peace.

Lord, this bosom's ardent feeling
Vainly would my lips express.
Low before Thy footstool kneeling,
Deign Thy suppliant's prayer to bless:
Let Thy grace, my soul's chief treasure,
Love's pure flame within me raise;
And, since words can never measure,
Let my life show forth Thy praise.

FRANCIS SCOTT KEY Baltimore, Maryland, 1823 *Episcopal*

Key is best known for writing "The Star-Spangled Banner" after watching the bombardment of Fort McHenry by the British in the War of 1812, and seeing through the smoke the following morning that the ramparts were still flying the American flag. He was the son of a Revolutionary officer and was a successful trial lawyer who at one time served as the U.S. District Attorney. One of Key's many illustrious descendants was F. Scott Fitzgerald, who proudly carried his name.

Key's secular success did not overshadow his religious life—indeed, he nearly gave up law to enter the ministry. A good example of Key's belief can be found in the following excerpt, in which he used his skills as a lawyer to defend his own faith after a friend's was shaken by reading Voltaire: "Men may argue ingeniously against our faith, as indeed they may against anything—but what can they say in defense of their own—I would carry the war into their own territories, I would ask them what they believe—if they said they believed anything, I think that they might be shown to be more full of difficulties and liable to infinitely greater objections than the system they oppose and they were credulous and unreasonable for believing it. If they said they did not believe anything, you could not, to be sure, have anything further to say to them. In that case they would be insane, or at best ill-qualified to teach others what they ought to believe or disbelieve." The last line of this hymn served as Key's public—and private—motto.

The Perfect World, By Adam Trod

Where wast thou when I laid the foundations of the earth? declare, if thou hast understanding. Who hath laid the measures thereof, if thou knowest? or who hath stretched the line upon it? Whereupon are the foundations thereof fastened? or who laid the corner stone thereof; When the morning stars sang together, and all the sons of God shouted for joy? —Job 38:4–7

The perfect world, by Adam trod,
Was the first temple built by God;
His fiat laid the corner stone,
And heaved its pillars, one by one.

He hung its starry roof on high,
The broad expanse of azure sky;
He spread its pavement, green and bright,
And curtained it with morning light.

The mountains in their places stood,
The sea, the sky; and all was good;
And when its first pure praises rang,
The morning stars together sang.

Lord, 'tis not ours to make the sea,
And earth, and sky, a house for thee;
But in thy sight our offering stands,
A humbler temple, made with hands.

NATHANIEL PARKER WILLIS New Haven, Connecticut, 1826 *Unitarian*
Willis was from a long line of religious figures, publishers, and printers, and was himself a respected magazine editor, journalist, and poet on sacred themes. A controversial figure in New York society, he posed for Mathew Brady's camera and was an acquaintance of Walt Whitman, a foe of Henry Wadsworth Longfellow, and an enemy, and then friend, of Edgar Allan Poe. Willis and Poe exchanged barbed reviews of each other's work, taking witty stabs at one another until each man grew in the other's estimation. Willis eventually hired Poe to work at his magazine, and went on to be the first to publish "The Raven." He mentored other aspiring writers, including William Thackeray.

Willis wrote this hymn the year he graduated from Yale, in honor of the consecration of the Hanover Street Church in Boston. The Edenic setting of the hymn foreshadows Willis's later talent for describing his surroundings in travelogues as "written pictures."

Go Down, Moses

And the Lord spake unto Moses, Go unto Pharaoh, and say unto him, Thus saith the Lord, Let my people go, that they may serve me. —Exodus 8:1

When Israel was in Egypt's land:
Let my people go,
Oppress'd so hard they could not stand
Let my people go.

Go down, Moses,
Away down in Egypt land,
And tell King Pharaoh,
To let my people go.

Thus saith the Lord, bold Moses said,
Let my people go;
If not I'll smite your first-born dead,
Let my people go.

No more shall they in bondage toil,
Let my people go;
Let them come out with Egypt's spoil,
Let my people go.

Then Israel out of Egypt came,
Let my people go;
And left the proud oppressive land,
Let my people go.

'Twas good old Moses and Aaron, too,
Let my people go;
'Twas they that led the armies through,
Let my people go.

O come along Moses, you'll not get lost,
Let my people go;
Stretch out your rod and come across,
Let my people go.

As Israel stood by the waterside,
Let my people go;
At the command of God it did divide,
Let my people go.

O let us all from bondage flee,
Let my people go;
And let us all in Christ be free
Let my people go.

TRADITIONAL SPIRITUAL

One of the first published spirituals, "Go Down, Moses" was transcribed from the song of escaped slaves who gathered at Fortress Monroe in Hampton, Virginia, during the Union army's occupation in 1861. It appeared in the *New York Tribune* that December, and within two weeks was published as sheet music. Harriet Tubman, called the Moses of her people, used this as a rallying song. It was also one of the songs performed by the Jubilee Singers of Fisk University—all former slaves or children of slaves who went on tour to raise funds for the university, founded in 1866 to offer education to the newly freed.

The best known of all spirituals or "sorrow songs," it is a powerful example of the fusion of African musical styles—including call and response (where a leader sings or chants a few lines, followed by the group's repetition or variations on the lines in response), rich harmonies, and improvisation—with the biblical stories that were introduced by Christian missionaries and during services on plantations. Following Lincoln's Emancipation Proclamation in 1862, a new verse was sung: "Go down, Abraham / Away down in Dixie's land; / Tell Jeff Davis / To let my people go."

The Hour-Glass

Ye also, as lively stones, are built up a spiritual house, an holy priesthood, to offer up spiritual sacrifices, acceptable to God by Jesus Christ. —1 Peter 2:5

Alas! how swift the moments fly!
How flash the years along!
Scarce here, yet gone already by,
The burden of a song.
See childhood, youth, and manhood pass,
And age, with furrowed brow;
Time was—Time shall be—drain the glass—
But where in Time is *now?*

Time is the measure but of change;
No present hour is found;
The past, the future, fill the range
Of Time's unceasing round.
Where, then is *now?* In realms above,
With God's atoning Lamb,
In regions of eternal love,
Where sits enthroned I AM.

Then pilgrim, let thy joys and tears
On Time no longer lean;
But henceforth all thy hopes and fears
From earth's affections wean:
To God let votive accents rise;
With truth, with virtue, live;
So all the bliss that Time denies
Eternity shall give.

JOHN QUINCY ADAMS Plymouth, Massachusetts, 1839 *Unitarian*
Son of the second president of the United States, Adams served most of his adult life in public office as an ambassador, senator, and U.S. congressman in addition to being the sixth president. He was a spiritual man who read the Bible from cover to cover each year, an hour each day after rising, but who supported the separation of church and state by opposing attempts to make Sunday a mandatory day of rest. He defended women's rights of representation in government by citing biblical stories to a congressman who suggested that politically active women would better serve their nation through domestic duties: "Where did the gentleman get this principle? Has he forgotten Esther, who by her petition saved her people and her country?" Adams's most famous humanitarian effort while in office was against slavery. In 1841 he successfully defended the thirty-six slaves who mutinied aboard the Spanish slave ship *Amistad* in the Caribbean.

   This hymn was written for the occasion of the 200th anniversary of the First Congregational Church in Quincy, Massachusetts, the church of his family. Adams was a cofounder of the First Unitarian Church in Washington, D.C., although he was never in complete agreement with their beliefs, particularly regarding the divinity of Christ, which he recognized.

O Where Are Kings and Empires Now

The grass withereth, the flower fadeth: but the word of our God shall stand for ever. — Isaiah 40:8

O where are kings and empires now
Of old, that went and came?
But Lord, Thy Church is praying yet,
A thousand years the same.

We mark her goodly battlements
And her foundations strong;
We hear, within, the solemn voice
Of her unending song.

For not like kingdoms of the world
Thy holy Church, O God!
Though earthquake shocks are threat'ning her,
And tempests are abroad;

Unshaken as eternal hills,
Immovable she stands,
A mountain that shall fill the earth,
A house not made by hands.

ARTHUR CLEVELAND COXE New York, New York, 1839 *Episcopal*

Son of a well-known Presbyterian minister, Coxe was the bishop of western New York for the Episcopal Church, and was also a part of the Hymnal Commission that prepared the official collection of hymns for his church in 1869. As part of that board, he humbly refused the inclusion of his own works. He wrote a number of small volumes of poetry; this hymn was written before his ordination in 1842.

Ironically, America at this time was expanding its own empire, propelled by the ideal of Manifest Destiny. In the name of progress, Americans claimed southern and western territories, forcing 15,000 Cherokee to march a thousand miles from their land in Georgia to Oklahoma on the Trail of Tears; 4,000 died as a result of President Andrew Jackson's Indian Removal Act. Many Americans opposed these atrocities, including Tennessee congressman Davy Crockett, who supported the Cherokee and destroyed his political career in the process. He went west to Texas, saying, "I would sooner be honestly damned than hypocritically immortalized." Still, after two thousand years of war and peace, Coxe's words ring true: the churches *do* still stand, and pray, and sing.

Nearer, My God, to Thee

And he lighted upon a certain place, and tarried there all night, because the sun was set; and he took of the stones of that place, and put them for his pillows, and lay down in that place to sleep. And he dreamed, and behold a ladder set up on the earth, and the top of it reached to heaven: and behold the angels of God ascending and descending on it. —Genesis 28:11–12

Nearer, my God, to thee,
Nearer to thee!
E'en tho' it be a cross
That raiseth me!
Still all my song would be,
Nearer, my God, to thee—
Nearer to thee!

Tho' like the wanderer,
The sun gone down,
Darkness be over me,
My rest a stone;
Yet in my dreams I'd be
Nearer, my God, to thee—
Nearer to thee!

There let the way appear
Steps unto heaven;
All that thou send'st to me
In mercy given;
Angels to beckon me
Nearer, my God, to thee—
Nearer to thee!

Then with my waking thoughts,
Bright with thy praise,
Out of my stony griefs
Bethel I'll raise;
So by my woes to be
Nearer, my God, to thee—
Nearer to thee!

Or if on joyful wing
Cleaving the sky,
Sun, moon, and stars forgot,
Upwards I fly:
Still all my song shall be,
Nearer, my God, to thee—
Nearer to thee!

SARAH FLOWER ADAMS London, England, 1840 *Unitarian*
Adams was the daughter of a liberal publisher and journalist who was imprisoned for his articles criticizing the politics of an Anglican bishop. She was unusual in her time for her feminist and political activism. She was married to an equally liberal inventor and political author, with whom she had a premarital agreement that she would do no housework. A poet and literary critic of the romantic school, Adams was one of the growing cadre of recognized female authors, including Christina Rossetti, the Brontë sisters, Jane Austen, and Elizabeth Barrett Browning, although most of her own poetry would not be published until after her death. Her immediate literary circle included Percy Shelley and Robert Browning. She wrote this hymn for the Unitarians at Finsbury, whose pastor, George Fox, was known for his vigorous reform efforts for women's rights and a free press. The music was written by Adams's sister, Eliza Flower.

The first three lines of this hymn were the dying words of President McKinley following his 1901 assassination. As part of the country's mourning, it was sung the following Sunday in churches nationwide.

Believe Not Those Who Say

Also now, behold, my witness is in heaven, and my record is on high. My friends scorn me: but mine eye poureth out tears unto God. —Job 16:19–20

Believe not those who say
The upward path is smooth,
Lest thou should stumble in the way,
And faint before the truth.

To labor and to love,
To pardon and endure,
To lift thy heart to God above,
And keep thy conscience pure.

Be this thy constant aim,
Thy hope, thy chief delight,
What matter who should whisper blame
Or who should scorn or slight.

Anne Brontë Haworth, England, before 1847 *Anglican Evangelical*
Raised by a severe evangelical Anglican pastor and a Methodist aunt, Anne was the youngest and most spiritual of the three famous sisters. The Brontë girls were raised in a town that seventy years before had hosted John Wesley's sermons on numerous occasions. Anne spent many hours seeking guidance on the topic of salvation—not from her father, but from a Moravian minister. She apparently denied the concept of eternal damnation, and of the spiritually elect, instead believing that all will be saved; in this, she was more akin to Universalists than Methodists or Anglicans. She called her poems her "pillars of witness."

A Little Kingdom I Possess

And when he was demanded of the Pharisees, when the kingdom of God should come, he answered them and said, The kingdom of God cometh not with observation: Neither shall they say, Lo here! or, Lo there! for, behold, the kingdom of God is within you. —Luke 17:20–21

A little kingdom I possess,
Where thoughts and feelings dwell,
And very hard the task I find
Of governing it well.
For passion tempts and troubles me,
A wayward will misleads,
And selfishness its shadow casts,
On all my words and deeds.

How can I learn to rule myself,
To be the child I should,
Honest and brave, and never tire
Of trying to be good?
How can I keep a sunny soul
To shine along life's way?
How can I tune my little heart,
To sweetly sing all day?

Dear Father, help me with the love
That castesth out my fear!
Teach me to lean on Thee and feel
That thou art very near.
That no temptation is unseen,
No childish grief too small,
Since Thou, with patience infinite,
Doth soothe and comfort all.

I do not ask for any crown
But that which all may win;
Nor try to conquer any world
Except the one within.
Be Thou my Guide until I find,
Led by a tender hand,
Thy happy kingdom in myself
And dare to take command.

LOUISA MAY ALCOTT Concord, Massachusetts, 1846
The author of *Little Women* was the daughter of the brilliant educator, philosopher, and abolitionist Bronson Alcott. As a child, Louisa studied in Ralph Waldo Emerson's library and was given botany instruction by Henry David Thoreau, both friends of her father's. She was also worked harder than most children, both physically and intellectually. Her father cofounded a utopian community called Fruitlands when Louisa was ten, leading a small group of families who lived as vegetarians and discussed philosophy, working the land by hand with no beasts of burden save themselves—usually, the women and children.

Alcott traced her spiritual development from her childhood when she ran through the Concord woods in autumn and stopped to see the sun falling across the meadows as the pines rustled around her: "It seemed as if I felt God as I never did before, and I prayed in my heart that I might keep that happy sense of nearness all my life." Alcott had a personal relationship with God, and while she never joined a congregation, she did enjoy Unitarian sermons. Written when she was just thirteen, and the only hymn she penned in a long, varied career as both author and advocate, these words gave her comfort throughout her life.

Simple Gifts

Now there are diversities of gifts, but the same Spirit. — 1 Corinthians 12:4

'Tis the gift to be simple,'tis the gift to be free,
'Tis the gift to come down where we ought to be;
And when we find ourselves in the place just right,
'Twill be in the valley of love and delight.

When true simplicity is gain'd,
To bow and to bend we shan't be asham'd
To turn, turn will be our delight,
'Till by turning, turning we come round right.

ELDER JOSEPH BRACKETT (attributed) Alfred, Maine, 1848 *Shaker*
Elder Brackett lived during a period of spiritualist phenomena in the Shaker communities which included "Gift Songs." Members experienced visitations from Mother Ann Lee, their founder, as well as God, Jesus, and a host of native spirits, who transmitted to them sacred lyric poems and ideas for paintings. These visits came in dream and trance states, after which people spoke of journeys and conversations with these entities; more than 10,000 hymns and songs were "given" as spiritual gifts in this period. Some records indicate that "Simple Gifts," too, was given by a spirit, that of a slave boy.

Shaker men and women lived separate—but equal—celibate lives, meeting only for prayer services and dances. Technically this is a "quick dance," not a hymn, as it includes no scriptural references. The "turning" mentioned in the lyrics was mirrored in dancing, with skirts and coattails spinning—turning from worldliness, sin, and selfishness, turning toward simplicity, community, and God. Shakers crafted their verse with the same care that they gave their famous woodwork. This song offered the theme for Aaron Copland's 1944 ballet suite *Appalachian Spring*, was recorded by Judy Collins, and was sung at President Clinton's first inauguration.

It Came upon the Midnight Clear

And suddenly there was with the angel a multitude of the heavenly host praising God, and saying, Glory to God in the highest, and on earth peace, good will toward men. —Luke 2:13–14

It came upon the midnight clear—
That glorious song of old,
From angels bending near the earth
To touch their harps of gold:
"Peace on the earth, good will to men
From heaven's all-gracious King!"
The world in solemn stillness lay
To hear the angels sing.

Still through the cloven skies they come,
With heavenly wing unfurled,
And still their heavenly music floats
O'er all the weary world;
Above its sad and lonely plains
They bend on hovering wing,
And ever o'er its Babel sounds
The blessed angels sing.

Yet with the woes of sin and strife
The world has suffered long;
Beneath the angels' strain have rolled
Two thousand years of wrong;
And man, at war with man, hears not
The love song which they bring:
O hush the noise, ye men of strife,
And hear the angels sing!

And ye, beneath life's crushing load,
Whose forms are bending low,
Who toil along the climbing way
With painful steps and slow,
Look now, for glad and golden hours
Come swiftly on the wing:
O rest beside the weary road,
And hear the angels sing!

For lo! the days are hastening on
By prophet bards foretold
When with the ever-circling years
Comes round the age of gold;
When peace shall over all the earth
Its ancient splendors fling,
And the whole world give back the song
Which now the angels sing.

Edmund Hamilton Sears Wayland, Massachusetts, 1849 *Unitarian*
Sears was a Unitarian minister as well as editor, author, and poet. He varied from most Unitarians, however, by accepting the divinity of Christ. "The word God may be uttered without emotion," he told his congregation, "while the word Jesus opens the heart, and touches the place of tears." His writings, which stressed the social responsibilities the Gospel teaches, were popular with liberal Protestants of many denominations.

   While Sears wrote this poem, the war with Mexico over Texas (and beyond) weighed heavily on him; he believed that to kill in war was as grievous a sin as murder. His text serves well beyond the Christmas season as an ethical acknowledgment of suffering, as well as the presence of hope, in the contemporary world.

Every Time I Feel the Spirit

Likewise the Spirit also helpeth our infirmities: for we know not what we should pray for as we ought: but the Spirit itself maketh intercession for us with groanings which cannot be uttered. —Romans 8:26

Upon a mountain my Lord spoke
Out of his mouth came fire and smoke
Down in the valley on my knees
I asked the Lord have mercy please

Every time I feel the spirit
Moving in my heart I will pray
Every time I feel the spirit
Moving in my heart I will pray

Jordan river chilly and cold
Chills my body but not my soul
All around me looking so fine
I ask the Lord and know it is mine

Every time I feel the spirit
Moving in my heart I will pray
Every time I feel the spirit
Moving in my heart I will pray

Ain't but one train runs this track
Runs to heaven runs right back
St. Peter waiting at the gate
Saying come on sinner, don't be late

Every time I feel the spirit
Moving in my heart I will pray
Every time I feel the spirit
Moving in my heart I will pray

Sinner, don't be late
Sinner, don't be late
Sinner, don't be late
Sinner, don't be late

Every time I feel the spirit
Moving in my heart I will pray
Every time I feel the spirit
Moving in my heart I will pray

TRADITIONAL SPIRITUAL

Slaves incorporated symbolic elements in their worship songs to relay messages from field to field, and plantation to plantation, without raising suspicions. As with "Go Down, Moses," biblical allusions serve as coded language in this song. The newly laid railway system that was opening up the Western territories represented their own paths to freedom as they escaped along the Underground Railroad. The rail lines first ran cargo and passengers in 1830, replacing the less efficient network of canals. During the Civil War, the railways carried troops to decisive battles like Bull Run. By 1869, the tracks ran from coast to coast.

Quakers and other abolitionists helped facilitate slave escapes as early as the eighteenth century, but the 1850 Fugitive Slave Bill made the penalty for this severe, so a greater degree of organization—and secrecy—became necessary. The Underground Railroad rolled through forests and fields, leading slaves to freedom north as far as Canada and south to Mexico with "conductors" like Harriet Tubman. An estimated one hundred thousand people are believed to have made their ways to cities like Chicago, Boston, New York, and Philadelphia along its paths.

Ring out the Old, Ring in the New

Therefore if any man be in Christ, he is a new creature: old things are passed away; behold, all things are become new.
—2 Corinthians 5:17

Ring out the old, ring in the new,
Ring, happy bells, across the snow:
The year is going, let him go;
Ring out the false, ring in the true.

Ring out, wild bells, to the wild sky,
The flying cloud, the frosty light:
The year is dying in the night;
Ring out, wild bells, and let him die.

Ring out the grief that saps the mind,
For those that here we see no more;
Ring out the feud of rich and poor,
Ring in redress to all mankind.

Ring out a slowly dying cause,
And ancient forms of party strife;
Ring in the nobler modes of life,
With sweeter manners, purer laws.

Ring out false pride in place and blood,
The civic slander and the spite;
Ring in the love of truth and right,
Ring in the common love of good.

Ring out old shapes of foul disease;
Ring out the narrowing lust of gold;
Ring out the thousand wars of old,
Ring in the thousand years of peace.

Ring in the valiant man and free,
The larger heart, the kindlier hand;
Ring out the darkness of the land,
Ring in the Christ that is to be.

ALFRED, LORD TENNYSON Shawell, England, 1850

The Tennyson family was plagued by what the poet called "black blood"—an inherited form of epilepsy that in the nineteenth century was mistaken for madness. Tennyson's father, a minister, and his brother suffered from the condition, as did he. He escaped this bleak atmosphere by joining two other brothers at Cambridge University and by becoming a member of a debating group called The Apostles, a gathering of earnest young men who sought to convert people to a social creed of awareness and service to others.

One of Tennyson's closest friends, Arthur Hallam, was exceptionally witty and charming; he was also one of the first supporters of Tennyson's poetry and was later engaged to the poet's sister Emily. The young man died tragically at twenty-three, leaving Tennyson reeling—and writing—for the next seventeen years. The result was "In Memoriam," considered Tennyson's finest poem. Published anonymously at first, it went on to make his reputation, selling well to all walks of life, including Queen Victoria's consort Prince Albert, and earned him the post of poet laureate, as well as the conference of a knighthood. The elegaic poem, which includes the text of this hymn, is a vivid exploration of the emotional and spiritual impacts of a loved one's death; of sorrow, accompanied by hope. In Tennyson's words: "fear, doubts, and suffering will find answer and relief only through Faith in a God of Love." Yet human love, too, gave the poet comfort. He once said of his wife, "The peace of God came into my life when I married her."

Good King Wenceslas

But to do good and to communicate forget not: for with such sacrifices God is well pleased. —Hebrews 13:16

Good King Wenceslas looked out,
On the Feast of Stephen,
When the snow lay round about,
Deep and crisp and even;
Brightly shone the moon that night,
Though the frost was cruel,
When a poor man came in sight,
Gath'ring winter fuel.

"Hither, page, and stand by me,
If thou know'st it, telling,
Yonder peasant, who is he?
Where and what his dwelling?"
"Sire, he lives a good league hence,
Underneath the mountain,
Right against the forest fence,
By Saint Agnes' fountain."

"Bring me flesh and bring me wine,
Bring me pine logs hither:
Thou and I will see him dine,
When we bear them thither."

Page and monarch, forth they went,
Forth they went together,
Through the cold wind's rude lament
And the bitter weather.

"Sire, the night is darker now,
And the wind blows stronger;
Fails my heart, I know not how;
I can go no longer."
"Mark my footsteps, my good page;
Tread thou in them boldly,
Thou shalt find the winter's rage
Freeze thy blood less coldly."

In his master's steps he trod,
Where the snow lay dinted;
Heat was in the very sod
Which the saint had printed.
Therefore, Christian men, be sure,
Wealth or rank possessing,
Ye who now will bless the poor
Shall yourselves find blessing.

JOHN MASON NEALE East Grinstead, England, prior to 1853 *Anglican*
Neale, a clergyman, supported the Oxford Movement, which sought to restore Roman rituals to the Anglican mass. His contribution came mainly in the form of fifteen volumes of poetic translations of ancient and medieval Greek and Latin hymns for use by the Church of England, including "O Come, O Come, Emmanuel."
    Neale wrote this original hymn, however, to honor the feast day of the martyr St. Stephen on December 26. Stephen was one of seven men ordained by the Apostles to oversee the giving of alms to the poor; in England, December 26, Boxing Day, was traditionally a day for all to share their plenty with the less fortunate. Neale chose the Bohemian martyr Wenceslas for his theme, as St. Stephen and the duke (he was not actually a king) shared not only dying for their faith and later canonization, but also reputations for service to the needy. Wenceslas was recognized as a saint as early as the eleventh century. Since his death, many legends of his kind and miraculous actions have shrouded his memory—including one of a page and poor man.

What a Friend We Have in Jesus

Henceforth I call you not servants; for the servant knoweth not what his lord doeth: but I have called you friends; for all things that I have heard of my Father I have made known unto you. —John 15:15

What a Friend we have in Jesus,
All our sins and griefs to bear;
What a privilege to carry everything
To God in prayer.
Oh what peace we often forfeit,
Oh what needless pain we bear,
All because we do not carry
Everything to God in prayer.

Have we trials and temptations?
Is there trouble anywhere?
We should never be discouraged;
Take it to the Lord in prayer.
Can we find a Friend so faithful
Who will all our sorrows share?
Jesus knows our every weakness;
Take it to the Lord in prayer.

Are we weak and heavy laden,
Cumbered with a load of care?
Precious Savior, still our refuge,
Take it to the Lord in prayer.
Do your friends despise, forsake you?
Take it to the Lord in prayer.
In His arms He'll take and shield you;
You will find a solace there.

JOSEPH MEDLICOTT SCRIVEN Port Hope, Ontario, 1855 *Plymouth Brethren*

Scriven's life reads like a Victorian tragedy. Born in Ireland, he was educated at Trinity College, and his life seemed set on course until the drowning of his fiancée the night before their wedding. He turned to the principles of the Plymouth Brethren, an Anglo-Irish evangelical group whose founders were known for giving away their considerable fortunes to tenants and the needy, and creating a non-denominational following with an emphasis on biblical infallibility, premillennial "end of days" prophecy, and a de-emphasis on central authority. Each group was independent, each individual was both minister and congregant. The group is seen as the origin of Christian fundamentalism.

Following their example, Scriven donated his worldly possessions to the poor in Ireland before immigrating to Canada. Once on new ground, he walked around with a saw, cutting firewood for the poor and doing other good works anonymously. He tutored to earn a humble living, but heartache came again with the death of his second fiancée, this time from pneumonia. This hymn was written as a poem he called "Pray Without Ceasing" to comfort his mother through a troubling time in Ireland. Scriven had no intention of publishing it, and when a friend happened upon the original, Scriven only said, "The Lord and I did it between us." It was published shortly after Scriven's own death by drowning. Its expression is evidence of the growing movement toward viewing Christ as a daily comfort and present joy in one's life rather than a distant religious figure, and is historically one of the first songs taught to converts.

The Voice That Breathed o'er Eden

For this cause shall a man leave his father and mother, and shall be joined unto his wife, and they two shall be one flesh.
—Ephesians 5:31

The voice that breathed o'er Eden,
That earliest wedding day,
The primal wedding blessing,
It hath not passed away.

Still in the pure espousal
Of Christian man and maid
The Holy Three are with us,
The threefold grace is said.

For dower of blessèd children,
For love and faith's sweet sake,
For high mysterious union,
Which naught on earth may break.

Be present, loving Father,
To give away this bride,
As Eve Thou gav'st to Adam,
Out of his own pierced side:

Be present, Son of Mary,
To join their loving hands
As thou didst bind two natures
In thine eternal bands.

Be present, Holiest Spirit,
To bless them as they kneel,
As thou for Christ, the Bridegroom,
The Heavenly Spouse dost seal.

O, spread Thy pure wing o'er them,
Let no ill power find place
When onward to Thine altar
The hallowed path they trace,

To cast their crowns before Thee
In perfect sacrifice,
Till to the home of gladness
With Christ's own Bride they rise.

JOHN KEBLE Hursley, England, 1857 *Anglican*
Keble was an Anglican priest, a theologian, and a poet as well as an Oxford professor of poetry; his *The Christian Year: Thoughts in Verse for the Sundays and Holydays Throughout the Year* went through ninety-six editions in his lifetime. Keble initiated the Oxford Movement series of high church reforms for the Church of England that would have as significant an impact on nineteenth-century Great Britian as Methodism had in the eighteenth. The prime minister in 1833 had instructed the bishops of the Church of England "to set their house in order" after only six people had attended Easter services in St. Paul's Cathedral in London. The splintering evangelical groups had claimed many members—Congregational, Methodist, and Baptist missionaries had all drawn converts away from England's official church for the last hundred years. The Oxford Movement held that the church had strayed too far from its Catholic roots, and that Methodists and other dissenters preached false doctrines, and so Keble and others (including fellow hymnist John Neale and future prime minister William Gladstone) sought to reinvigorate the church by reinstating ceremonial rituals and doctrines of Roman Catholic services. They introduced choirs to the Anglican churches, emphasized the importance of communion, and focused their energies on the plights of those living in cities, like the London so infamous in fellow Anglican Charles Dickens' *David Copperfield*.

We Three Kings of Orient Are

Now when Jesus was born in Bethlehem of Judaea in the days of Herod the king, behold, there came wise men from the east to Jerusalem, Saying, Where is he that is born King of the Jews? for we have seen his star in the east, and are come to worship him.— Matthew 2:1–2

We three kings of Orient are;
Bearing gifts we traverse afar,
Field and fountain,
Moor and mountain,
Following yonder star.

O Star of Wonder, Star of Night,
Star with Royal Beauty bright,
Westward leading,
Still proceeding,
Guide us to thy perfect Light.

Born a King on Bethlehem's plain
Gold I bring to crown Him again,
King for ever,
Ceasing never,
Over us all to reign.

Refrain

Frankincense to offer have I,
Incense owns a Deity nigh;
Prayer and praising,
All men raising,
Worship Him God on high.

Refrain

Myrrh is mine, its bitter perfume
Breathes a life of gathering gloom;—
Sorrowing, sighing,
Bleeding, dying,
Sealed in the stone-cold tomb.

Refrain

Glorious now behold Him arise,
King, and God, and Sacrifice;
Heaven sings
'Hallelujah':
'Hallelujah' the earth replies.

Refrain

JOHN HENRY HOPKINS JR. New York, New York, 1857 *Episcopal*
Son of an influential and musically gifted Episcopal bishop of Vermont, Hopkins followed in his father's footsteps by becoming a priest and music teacher at the General Theological Seminary in New York. He wrote this hymn for a Christmas pageant during his tenure there.

The tale of the three kings is one of the most legend-enhanced stories from the Bible. The Magi, or wise men as they are referred to in the Gospel of St. Matthew, are not named as they later were in the eighth century as Melchior, Gaspard, and Balthazar. The Magi were scholarly priests of the Persian (present-day Iran) Zoroastrian faith, highly esteemed not only for their knowledge of astronomy and other sciences, but also for their dream interpretations. Their (purported) remains rest in the cathedral in Cologne, Germany, which was built to house them after their eight-hundred-year stay in Constantinople. The day the Magi arrived in Bethlehem is traditionally held as January 6th, Epiphany, also known as Twelfth Night.

Again, As Evening's Shadow Falls

Behold, the hour cometh, yea, is now come, that ye shall be scattered, every man to his own, and shall leave me alone: and yet I am not alone, because the Father is with me. —John 16:32

Again, as evening's shadow falls,
We gather in these hallowed walls;
And vesper hymn and vesper prayer
Rise mingling on the holy air.

May struggling hearts that seek release
Here find the rest of God's own peace;
And, strengthened here by hymn and prayer,
Lay down the burden and the care.

O God, our Light! to Thee we bow;
Within all shadows standest Thou;
Give deeper calm than night can bring;
Give sweeter songs than lips can sing.

Life's tumult we must meet again,
We cannot at the shrine remain;
But in the spirit's secret cell
May hymn and prayer forever dwell!

SAMUEL LONGFELLOW Brooklyn, New York, 1859 *Unitarian*
Youngest brother of the poet Henry Wadsworth Longfellow, Samuel was a pastor and hymnologist, compiling two hymnals during his career. He was said to have the soul of a poet and the heart of a saint. He adapted the transcendentalist philosophies of Henry and other leading minds of the times, including Emerson and Thoreau, to his Unitarian sermons and hymns. The transcendentalists saw God in nature and in every man, and emphasized the knowledge that comes from intuition and self-reliance; they opposed traditional forms of authority in religious or secular affairs, at times taking this to its natural conclusion by living in separate utopian societies. The theme of holding onto the messages we receive in church, of understanding and appreciating God's omnipresence, is a lovely union of traditional Christian and transcendentalist beliefs.

Eternal Father, Strong to Save

Then they cry unto the Lord in their trouble, and he bringeth them out of their distresses. He maketh the storm a calm, so that the waves thereof are still. Then are they glad because they be quiet; so he bringeth them unto their desired haven.
—Psalm 107:28–30

Eternal Father, strong to save,
Whose arm doth bind the restless wave,
Who bidd'st the mighty ocean deep
Its own appointed limits keep:
Oh, hear us, when we cry to thee,
For those in peril on the sea.

O Saviour, whose almighty word
The winds and waves submissive heard,
Who walkedst on the foaming deep
And calm amidst its rage didst sleep;
Oh, hear us when we cry to thee
For those in peril on the sea.

O sacred Spirit, who didst brood
Upon the chaos dark and rude,
And bad'st its angry tumult cease
And gavest light and love and peace:
Oh, hear us when we cry to thee
For those in peril on the sea.

O Trinity of love and power,
Our brethren shield in danger's hour;
From rock and tempest, fire and foe,
Protect them wheresoe'er they go:
And ever let there rise to thee
Glad hymns of praise from land and sea.

WILLIAM WHITING Winchester, England, 1860 *Anglican*
Reverend Whiting was master of Winchester College Choristers' School; he wrote this poem for a student who was sailing to America, no doubt recalling an earlier voyage of his own on the storm-tossed Mediterranean. By the mid-nineteenth century, a steady stream of men, women, and children were emigrating from Europe to America; in the decade preceding Lincoln's presidency, 2.5 million people from Great Britain, Ireland, and Germany arrived on North Atlantic shores to fill manual labor positions in the rising industries, while many more Chinese and Japanese arrived on the Pacific coast following the expansion of the railways and discovery of gold—all of them braving long, uncomfortable trips over rough seas.

Also known as "The Navy Hymn" following its adoption for Sunday services by the U.S. Naval Academy Midshipman's Choir, this was the favorite hymn of Presidents Theodore Roosevelt (former secretary of the Navy) and Franklin Delano Roosevelt (former assistant secretary of the Navy). It was performed as the body of President John F. Kennedy (a World War II PT boat commander) was brought to lie in state at the U.S. Capitol. Over the years, new verses have been added as prayers of protection for pilots, submarine crews, Antarctic scientists, and astronauts. It is also sung by Great Britian's Royal Navy and by the French navy.

Even Me

Lord, I hear of showers of blessing
Thou art scattering full and free;
Showers the thirsty land refreshing;
Let some drops now fall on me;
Even me, even me,
Let some drops now fall on me.

Pass me not, O gracious Father!
Sinful though my heart may be;
Thou might'st curse me, but the rather
Let Thy mercy light on me;
Even me, even me,
Let Thy mercy light on me.

Pass me not, O tender Savior!
Let me love and cling to Thee;
I am longing for Thy favour;
When thou comest, call for me,
Even me, even me,
When thou comest, call for me.

Pass me not, O mighty Spirit!
Thou canst make the blind to see;
Witnesser of Jesus' merit,
Speak the word of power to me;
Even me, even me,
Speak the word of power to me.

Have I been in sin long sleeping,
Long been slighting, grieving Thee?
Has the world my heart been keeping?
O forgive and rescue me;
Even me, even me,
O forgive and rescue me.

Love of God, so pure and changeless,
Blood of Christ, so rich and free;
Grace of God, so strong and boundless,
Magnify them all in me;
Even me, even me,
Magnify them all in me.

Pass me not; this lost one bringing,
Bind my heart, O Lord, to Thee;
All my heart to thee is springing,
Blessing others, O bless me;
Even me, even me,
Blessing others, O bless me.

ELIZABETH CODNER London, England, 1860 *Anglican Independent*
Codner was a minister's wife who devoted much of her energy to missionary efforts. She worked alongside William Pennefather, a hymnist and the founder of the Mildmay Protestant Mission, and edited the Mildmay monthly magazine *Woman's Work in the Great Harvest Field.* One of the many positive ancillary effects of mission work, along with the founding of hospitals and orphanages (building on the tradition established by the Jews and Catholics), was that it offered women a respectable alternative to being housewives, teachers, or governesses. Women traveled the world and rolled up their sleeves side-by-side with men, proving their mettle and usefulness in an era that was otherwise quite limiting for professional women.

I Heard the Bells on Christmas Day

Hope deferred maketh the heart sick: but when the desire cometh, it is a tree of life. —Proverbs 13:12

I heard the bells on Christmas Day
Their old, familiar carols play,
And wild and sweet
The words repeat
Of peace on earth, good will to men!

And thought how, as the day had come,
The belfries of all Christendom
Had rolled along
The unbroken song
Of peace on earth, good will to men!

Till ringing, singing on its way
The world revolved from night to day,
A voice, a chime,
A chant sublime
Of peace on earth, good will to men!

Then from each black accursed mouth
The cannon thundered in the South,
And with the sound
The carols drowned
Of peace on earth, good will to men!

It was as if an earthquake rent
The hearth-stones of a continent,
And made forlorn
The households born
Of peace on earth, good will to men!

And in despair I bowed my head
"There is no peace on earth," I said,
"For hate is strong,
And mocks the song
Of peace on earth, good will to men!"

Then pealed the bells more loud and deep:
"God is not dead, nor doth he sleep!
The wrong shall fail,
The right prevail,
With peace on earth, good will to men!"

HENRY WADSWORTH LONGFELLOW Cambridge, Massachusetts, 1864 *Unitarian*
Brother of hymnist Samuel Longfellow, Henry Longfellow was part of the flowering of American arts in the mid-nineteenth century. He was a Harvard professor and an active abolitionist as well as an accomplished poet. By the time he wrote this hymn, he had already become famous as the best-selling author of the classic poems "Song of Hiawatha" and "The Courtship of Miles Standish."

But it was heartbreak that led him to write these verses, the fourth and fifth of which were usually omitted from hymnals, considered too bleak (and perhaps too political) for worship services. While still recovering from the tragic death by fire of his beloved wife Fanny, his son Charles, a Union lieutenant, was seriously wounded in battle in New Hope Church, Virginia, and was sent home for a slow and painful recovery. On Christmas Day 1863, the poet's journal exhibited his anxiety by an absence of entries, but a year later, his spirits had rallied along with his son's progress, and the ink flowed into the poem "Christmas Bells," which became this hymn.

Shall We Gather at the River?

And he shewed me a pure river of water of life, clear as crystal, proceeding out of the throne of God and of the Lamb.
—Revelation 22:1

Shall we gather at the river,
Where bright angel feet have trod,
With its crystal tide for ever
Flowing by the throne of God?
Yes, we'll gather at the river,
The beautiful, the beautiful river;
Gather with the saints at the river
That flows by the throne of God.

Ere we reach the shining river,
Lay we every burden down;
Grace our spirits will deliver,
And provide a robe and crown.
Yes, we'll gather at the river,
The beautiful, the beautiful river;
Gather with the saints at the river
That flows by the throne of God.

At the shining of the river,
Mirror of the Saviour's face,
Saints, whom death will never sever
Lift their song of saving grace.
Yes, we'll gather at the river,
The beautiful, the beautiful river;
Gather with the saints at the river
That flows by the throne of God.

Soon we'll reach the silver river,
Soon our pilgrimage will cease;
Soon our happy hearts will quiver
With the melodies of peace.
Yes, we'll gather at the river,
The beautiful, the beautiful river;
Gather with the saints at the river
That flows by the throne of God.

ROBERT WADSWORTH LOWRY Brooklyn, New York, 1864 *Baptist*
On a sweltering day in 1864, in the midst of a city-wide epidemic that was claiming many lives, Lowry, a pastor and professor of literature, lay motionless on a lounge in his study. As he was drowsy from the heat, his mind drifted, eventually landing upon the the life-giving qualities of rivers as described in Revelation. The poem was "born, not made," in Lowry's estimation, written in one fell swoop that afternoon. By the spring of 1865, the song had become so popular that Brooklyn's Sunday School Union hosted an event at which forty thousand children sang the words in parades and churches at the same time.

The enormous success of this and his other hymns, millions of copies of which were sold as sheet music, outshone Lowry's work as a pastor, which was a grave disappointment to him. He said, "I have always looked upon myself as a preacher and felt a sort of depreciation when I began to be known more as a composer." Although it was not Lowry's intent, the hymn was often sung at riverside immersion baptisms in more rural areas for decades after its composition. Of the hymn's success he wrote, "As a work of art, its author is not proud of it. As a hymn with power both to comfort and to inspire, he is glad to leave it as it is, performing its humble mission." Another of his works, "Where Is My Wandering Boy Tonight," while written from the experience of his son's disappearance, became a famous temperance hymn.

'Tis Winter Now, the Fallen Snow

For he saith to the snow, Be thou on the earth; likewise to the small rain, and to the great rain of his strength. —Job 37:6

'Tis winter now; the fallen snow
Has left the heav'ns all coldly clear;
Through leafless boughs the sharp winds blow,
And all the earth lies dead and drear.

And yet God's love is not withdrawn;
His life within the keen air breathes;
His beauty paints the crimson dawn,
And clothes the boughs with glittering wreaths.

And though abroad the sharp winds blow,
And skies are chill, and frosts are keen,
Home closer draws her circle now,
And warmer glows her light within.

O God, who giv'st the winters cold,
As well as sunbeams' joyous rays!
Us warmly in Thy love enfold,
And keep us through life's wintry days.

Samuel Longfellow Brooklyn, New York, 1864 *Unitarian*
By the winter of 1864, Abraham Lincoln had been reelected, but the Civil War still raged. Battlefield scenes arrived in homes on the pages of *Harper's Weekly,* illustrated by Thomas Nast and a young Winslow Homer. But in the midst of hope's "winter," Longfellow employed a romanticist's allegories of nature to affirm that God's presence remains, even in the darkest hours.

The Longfellows were surrounded by extraordinary literary talent. By the mid-nineteenth century, with one hundred years of explosive economic and population growth (and independence from Europe) behind the nation, American poets and authors began to rival those of Europe. Original language, new voices, and fresh literary forms began to emerge, including Edgar Allan Poe's *Tales of Mystery and Imagination,* Mark Twain's *Huckleberry Finn,* Herman Melville's *Moby Dick,* Emily Dickinson's poetry, and Walt Whitman's *Leaves of Grass.*

O Little Town of Bethlehem

But thou, Bethlehem Ephratah, though thou be little among the thousands of Judah, yet out of thee shall he come forth unto me that is to be ruler in Israel; whose goings forth have been from of old, from everlasting. —Micah 5:2

O little town of Bethlehem!
How still we see thee lie,
Above thy deep and dreamless sleep
The silent stars go by.
Yet in thy dark streets shineth
The Everlasting Light;
The hopes and fears of all the years
Are met in thee tonight.

For Christ is born of Mary,
And gathered all above,
While mortals sleep, the angels keep
Their watch of wondering love.
O morning stars together,
Proclaim the holy birth!
And praises sing to God the King,
And peace to men on earth.

How silently, how silently,
The wondrous gift is given;
So God imparts to human hearts
The blessings of his heaven.
No ear may hear his coming,
But in this world of sin,
Where meek souls will receive him still,
The dear Christ enters in.

O holy Child of Bethlehem!
Descend to us, we pray,
Cast out our sin and enter in,
Be born in us today.
We hear the Christmas angels
The great glad tidings tell;
O, come to us, abide with us,
Our Lord Emmanuel!

PHILLIPS BROOKS Philadelphia, Pennsylvania, 1868 *Episcopal*
Brooks was known as a "Prince of the Pulpit"—an engaging, well-read, and passionate speaker whose eager audiences included a wide range of people, including Queen Victoria and Helen Keller. Following a journey to Bethlehem for Christmas 1865, which included mass in the Church of the Nativity and a horseback ride by the Field of the Shepherds, Brooks formed a strong impression of what the moment of Christ's birth must have looked and felt like. He wrote this hymn for his Sunday school; for its premiere, it was sung by thirty-six children.

Christmas was not always a legal holiday, or even a religious one, as there is no date given for the Nativity in the Bible. Pope Julius set the date in 379 A.D. as December 25, but it wasn't until the nineteenth century that most American states recognized the holiday. The Puritans (including Brooks's ancestors) outlawed the celebration in the late seventeenth century, based, among other concerns, on lack of scriptural evidence of the date of the birth. Boston, until the latter half of the nineteenth century, still expected children at their school desks and workmen in their places on December 25.

Lord, Speak to Me

Only let your conversation be as it becometh the gospel of Christ: that whether I come and see you, or else be absent, I may hear of your affairs, that ye stand fast in one spirit, with one mind striving together for the faith of the gospel....
— Philippians 1:27

Lord, speak to me that I may speak
In living echoes of Thy tone;
As Thou has sought, so let me seek
Thine erring children lost and lone.

O lead me, Lord, that I may lead
The wandering and the wavering feet;
O feed me, Lord, that I may feed
Thy hungering ones with manna sweet.

O strengthen me, that while I stand
Firm on the Rock and strong in Thee,
I may stretch out a loving hand
To wrestlers with the troubled sea.

O teach me, Lord, that I may teach
The precious things Thou dost impart;
And wing my words, that they may reach
The hidden depths of many a heart.

O give Thine own sweet rest to me,
That I may speak with soothing power
A word in season, as from Thee,
To weary ones in needful hour.

O fill me with Thy fullness, Lord,
Until my very heart o'erflow
In kindling thought and glowing word,
Thy love to tell, Thy praise to show.

O use me, Lord, use even me,
Just *as* Thou wilt, and *when*, and *where*,
Until Thy blessèd Face I see,
Thy rest, Thy joy, Thy glory share.

FRANCES RIDLEY HAVERGAL Winterdyne, England, 1872 *Anglican Evangelical*
Havergal's father was an Anglican rector who influenced the daughter he nicknamed "Little Quicksilver" through his musicality and spirituality. He was the author of 100 hymns, but it is his daughter's compositions that have stood the test of time. Havergal was educated, charitable, cultured, and a fervent believer who was always mindful of her blessings. She wrote of her conversion, "When fifteen years old, I committed my soul to the Saviour, and earth and heaven seemed brighter from that moment." She began writing verse at seven and continued as a poet and hymnist until her early death at forty-two.

Havergal read the Bible daily, with Greek and Hebrew texts at hand as she went through making notes and underlining passages. She had a strict system of prayer on a piece of paper in her Bible that included reminders such as: "For Daily Morning Prayer: Watchfulness. Guard over temper. Consistency. Faithfulness to opportunities; Midday Prayer: Earnestness of spirit in desire, in prayer, and in all work; Evening Prayer: Forgiveness. To see my sinfulness in its true light." This hymn was first called "A Worker's Prayer."

Saved By Grace

And in that day shall the deaf hear the words of the book, and the eyes of the blind shall see out of obscurity, and out of darkness. — Isaiah 29:18

Some day the silver cord will break,
And I no more as now shall sing;
But O the joy when I shall wake
Within the palace of the King!

And I shall see Him face to face,
And tell the story — Saved by grace;
And I shall see Him face to face,
And tell the story — Saved by grace.

Some day my earthly house will fall.
I cannot tell how soon 'twill be;
But this I know — my All in All
Has now a place in heav'n for me.

And I shall see Him face to face,
And tell the story — Saved by grace;
And I shall see Him face to face,
And tell the story — Saved by grace.

Some day, when fades the golden sun
Beneath the rosy tinted west,
My blessèd Lord will say, "Well done!"
And I shall enter into rest.

And I shall see Him face to face,
And tell the story — Saved by grace;
And I shall see Him face to face,
And tell the story — Saved by grace.

Some day — till then I'll watch and wait,
My lamp all trimmed and burning bright,
That when my Savior opens the gate,
My soul to Him may take its flight.

And I shall see Him face to face,
And tell the story — Saved by grace;
And I shall see Him face to face,
And tell the story — Saved by grace.

FANNY CROSBY New York, New York, 1891 *Methodist Episcopal*
Crosby was blinded as a newborn through a doctor's negligence, but this author of more than 9,000 hymns not only overcame her physical adversity, she also succeeded as no female hymnist had before, and came to view her blindness as a blessing in disguise. Crosby's mother worked as a maid after her husband's death the year her daughter was born, leaving the baby in the care of her grandmother and a landlady who later gave her Bible lessons. Crosby was a student and then a teacher at the New York Institute for the Blind, but after marrying a fellow blind musician, she concentrated on hymn writing. Millions of her books of poetry and hymns were sold.

Of her thousands of songs, one was held back by Crosby for private devotion — "Saved By Grace," which she called her "soul's poem." She shared it publicly only after Ira Sankey, the famous evangelical musician, asked her to give a personal testimony. When another preacher later suggested that it was a pity that God had denied her sight when she had otherwise been so blessed, Crosby replied "Do you know that if at birth I had been able to make one petition, it would have been that I should be born blind?" When the gentleman asked why, she continued: "Because when I get to heaven, the first face that shall ever gladden my sight will be that of my Savior!"

America the Beautiful

Out of Zion, the perfection of beauty, God hath shined. —Psalm 50:2

O beautiful for spacious skies,
For amber waves of grain,
For purple mountain majesties
Above the fruited plain!
America! America!
God shed his grace on thee
And crown thy good with brotherhood
From sea to shining sea!

O beautiful for pilgrim feet
Whose stern, impassioned stress
A thoroughfare for freedom beat
Across the wilderness!
America! America!
God mend thine every flaw,
Confirm thy soul in self-control,
Thy liberty in law!

O beautiful for heroes proved
In liberating strife,
Who more than self their country loved,
And mercy more than life!
America! America!
May God thy gold refine
Till all success be nobleness
And every gain divine!

O beautiful for patriot dream
That sees beyond the years
Thine alabaster cities gleam
Undimmed by human tears!
America! America!
God shed His grace on thee
And crown thy good with brotherhood
From sea to shining sea!

KATHARINE LEE BATES Wellesley, Massachusetts, 1893 *Congregational*
Bates, the daughter of a Congregational pastor, was a poet as well as the chair of the literature department at Wellesley. In the summer of 1893, she traveled with some of her colleagues by train, wagon, and finally mule to the top of Pike's Peak in the Colorado Rockies. There, from the 14,000-foot viewpoint, she looked down at the grandeur before her, and the seeds of this famous, evocative hymn were planted. In her words, "when I saw the view, I felt great joy. All the wonder of America seemed displayed there, with the sea-like expanse." Bates attributed the last stanza to the many wonders of the "White City" at the Columbian Exposition in Chicago, which the group had visited en route west.

Bates wrote three versions of the hymn, changing her original lyrics of "Till selfish gain no longer stain / The banner of the free" to the less forceful "Till all success be nobleness / And every gain divine!" One of the best-loved of all American songs, Bates's work has been lobbied for as the national anthem on numerous occasions. While she received only a small check from its first publication in a weekly journal, she was pleased with its success, a testament, she believed, to the idealism and faith in human fellowship intrinsic in the American spirit. The song has been paired to more than sixty musical settings and recorded many times, by Elvis Presley and Ray Charles among countless others.

ALL CHRISTLY SOULS ARE ONE IN HIM
1900–Present

We intended gospel to strike a happy medium for the down-trodden. This music lifted people out of the muck and mire of poverty and loneliness, of being broke, and gave them some kind of hope anyway. —Thomas A. Dorsey

On Christmas Eve, 1906, Reg Fessenden, an inventor who had worked with Thomas Edison, broadcast a message to ships along the Atlantic seaboard via wireless telegraph. All the way from Brant Rock, Massachusetts, the sailors heard, for the first time in history, a voice and music carried magically through the air. Fessenden, the son of an Anglican minister, read from Luke's nativity text and played the nineteenth-century French carol "O Holy Night" on the violin, and a "new and glorious morn" had broken indeed.

The means by which Christian song was heard had changed a great deal since the days of monks chanting in Gothic cathedrals, itinerant ministers singing out into the hills from the saddle, and slaves hushing their voices inside groves of trees. The advent of radio signaled the beginning of mass communication. It is but one invention that revolutionized the reception of the Word of God; television and the Internet now give Christians a new and immediate way to fulfill the imperative of Mark 16:15: *And he said unto them, Go ye into all the world, and preach the gospel to every creature.* The best of the camp meeting revivalists could not have dreamed that someday millions of listeners around the world could be addressed at once.

In 1914, in the middle of the battles of World War I, a miraculous exchange of hymn singing inspired an informal truce. On the Western Front, the distance between the Axis and Allied troops was only sixty yards wide at some points; soldiers could see and hear the enemy clearly. But on Christmas morning, what was volleyed across No Man's Land from the German trenches was not rounds of bullets, but rounds of song. As one British soldier wrote, "They finished their carol and we thought that we ought to retaliate in some way, so we sang 'The First Noël,' and when we finished that they all began clapping; and then they struck up another favourite of theirs, 'O Tannenbaum.' And so it went on. First the Germans would sing one of their carols and then we would sing one of ours, until when we started up 'O Come All Ye Faithful' the Germans immediately joined in singing the same hymn to the Latin words 'Adeste Fidéles.' And I thought, well, this was really a most extraordinary thing—two nations both singing the same carol in the middle of a war."

One of the most significant strides in hymnody in the twentieth century was the contribution of African-Americans as individually recognized composers. Where the

86

Jubilee Singers had introduced spirituals created by generations of uncredited men and women to the listening public, now preacher-poets like Charles Tindley, the son of a slave, and Thomas A. Dorsey wrote gospel songs that married the best of accessible Christian messages with powerful music like the blues. Passed along, as spirituals had been before them, by word of mouth, as well as books and sheets that Tindley had printed privately, this compelling new sound of faith soon rang out in churches across the country.

It couldn't have come at a better time. At the turn of the century, 90 percent of African-Americans lived in southern states. But as the harsh realities of racism and the miseries of sharecropping became unbearable, many families—even whole parishes at a time—moved north to cities like Chicago and Philadelphia in the Great Migration. Once they arrived, however, the Great Depression severely limited their options, as it did people of every race and creed across the country. But where there was a church choir, or a radio station with a signal that reached them, people's minds and spirits were eased by singing gospel hymns.

But for all the comfort his words offered, Tindley didn't live to see his great works in the hymnal of his faith. It wasn't until 1964 that the Methodist hymnal carried just six African-American hymns, but his song had defiantly became a standard nonetheless. In this era of union and civil rights marches, the new protestants took Tindley's version of an old revival hymn, "I'll Overcome Some Day," and made it their own "We Shall Overcome." From the 1945 strike by the Negro Food and Tobacco Union in Charleston to the protests in Communist China's Tiananmen Square in 1989, and from the bus boycott led by Martin Luther King, Jr. to the Harlem Boys' and Girls' Choir's rendition at Yankee Stadium during the tribute to the victims of the September 11, 2001, terrorist attacks, this anthem has been heard around the world. When Tindley's hymns were finally included in the 1980 United Methodist supplemental songbook *Songs of Zion*, more than a million copies were sold.

Many great movements in society, both religious and secular, are galvanized by anthems. In the fourth century, Saint Ambrose sang hymns to calm and fortify Christians within a Milanese cathedral as heretics demanding the church for their own use marched outside. Fifteen centuries later, through world wars, cold wars, racial wars, and technology wars, hymns continue to help people fight society's, and their own, demons. Much remains to be healed, but history tells us that we shall overcome. And where there is hard work to be done, as we know from spirituals, singing helps—it is the rebellious triumph of the spirit over temporal concerns. And so we still "Lift every voice and sing, till earth and heaven ring, / Ring with the harmonies of liberty."

From Martin Luther to Martin Luther King, Jr., the faces and voices of praise and protest have changed, but the instincts remain the same: singing to understand, singing to be understood.

Lift Every Voice and Sing

O Zion, that bringest good tidings, get thee up into the high mountain; O Jerusalem, that bringest good tidings, lift up thy voice with strength; lift it up, be not afraid; say unto the cities of Judah, Behold your God! — Isaiah 40:9

Lift every voice and sing, till earth and heaven ring,
Ring with the harmonies of liberty;
Let our rejoicing rise, high as the listening skies,
Let it resound loud as the rolling sea.
Sing a song full of the faith that the dark past has taught us,
Sing a song full of the hope that the present has brought us;
Facing the rising sun of our new day begun,
Let us march on till victory is won.

Stony the road we trod, bitter the chastening rod,
Felt in the days when hope unborn had died;
Yet with a steady beat, have not our weary feet,
Come to the place for which our fathers sighed?
We have come over a way that with tears has been watered,
We have come treading our path through the blood of the slaughtered;
Out from the gloomy past, till now we stand at last
Where the white gleam of our bright star is cast.

God of our weary years, God of our silent tears,
Thou Who hast brought us thus far on our way;
Thou Who hast by Thy might, led us into the light,
Keep us forever in the path, we pray.
Lest our feet stray from the places, our God, where we met Thee.
Lest our hearts, drunk with the wine of the world, we forget Thee.
Shadowed beneath Thy hand, may we forever stand,
True to our God, true to our native land.

JAMES WELDON JOHNSON Jacksonville, Florida, 1900 *Baptist*
A songwriter, author, poet, lawyer, ambassador, professor, and civil rights leader, Johnson was masterful at all he endeavored. He was a man of precedent: the first black lawyer in the state of Florida; the first black newspaper publisher in the United States; and, with his brother, one of the first black songwriters for Broadway. Johnson was deeply influenced by tradition and his religious roots. His father, a gospel preacher, introduced him to the power and poetry of African religion. Within twenty years of the song's composition, this "Negro National Anthem" was sung in black schools throughout the South, its words pasted in the backs of songbooks and hymnals. Johnson was always amazed by the legend his hymn became. In 1935 he wrote, "The lines of this song repay me in elation, almost of exquisite anguish, whenever I hear them sung by Negro children."

I'll Overcome Some Day

Ye are of God, little children, and have overcome them: because greater is he that is in you, than he that is in the world.
—1 John 4:4

This world is one great battlefield
With forces all arrayed,
If in my heart I do not yield
I'll overcome some day.
I'll overcome some day,
I'll overcome some day,
If in my heart I do not yield,
I'll overcome some day.

Both seen and unseen powers join
To drive my soul astray,
But with His Word a sword of mine,
I'll overcome some day.
I'll overcome some day,
I'll overcome some day,
But with His Word a sword of mine,
I'll overcome some day.

A thousand snares are set for me,
And mountains in my way,
If Jesus will my leader be,
I'll overcome some day.
I'll overcome some day,
I'll overcome some day,
If Jesus will my leader be,
I'll overcome some day.

I fail so often when I try
My Savior to obey;
It pains my heart and then I cry,
Lord, make me strong some day.
Lord, make me strong some day,
Lord, make me strong some day;
It pains my heart and then I cry,
Lord, make me strong some day.

My mind is not to do the wrong,
But walk the narrow way;
I'm praying as I journey on,
To overcome some day.
To overcome some day,
To overcome some day;
I'm praying as I journey on,
To overcome some day.

Though many a time no signs appear,
Of answer when I pray;
My Jesus says I need not fear,
He'll make it plain some day.
I'll be like Him some day,
I'll be like Him some day;
My Jesus says I need not fear,
He'll make it plain some day.

CHARLES A. TINDLEY Philadelphia, Pennsylvania, 1900 *Methodist*
Born to an enslaved father and free mother, Tindley grew up working alongside slaves. He had no formal education, so he taught himself to read from scraps of newspapers, using the light from burning pine knots he patiently collected. Tindley went on to study theology (including Greek and Hebrew) through correspondence courses from Boston University School of Theology while working as a janitor in the church that would later become the Tindley Temple United Methodist Church, in Philadelphia. He was a riveting, rousing pastor, regularly filling the church with thousands of believers from many races and faiths. Tindley showed great understanding of his congregation's everyday trials and urged them to fight for their rights using nonviolent means. His hymns and sermons continue to inspire civil rights leaders around the world.

Be Thou My Vision

For he put on righteousness as a breastplate, and an helmet of salvation upon his head; and he put on the garments of vengeance for clothing, and was clad with zeal as a cloke. —Isaiah 59:17

Be Thou my Vision, O Lord of my heart,
Naught is all else to me, save that Thou art.
Thou my best thought, by day and by night,
Waking or sleeping, Thy presence my light.

Be thou my Wisdom, Thou my true Word,
I ever with thee, Thou with me, Lord.
Thou my great Father, I thy dear son,
Thou in me dwelling, I with thee one.

Be thou my breastplate, my sword for the fight,
Be Thou my dignity, Thy my delight.
Thou my soul's shelter, Thou my high tower,
Raise Thou me heavenward, Power of my power.

Riches I heed not, or man's empty praise,
Thou mine inheritance now and always.
Thou, and Thou only, first in my heart,
High King of Heaven, my treasure thou art.

With the High King of Heaven, after victory won,
May I reach Heaven's joys, O heaven's sun!
Heart of my own heart, whatever befall,
Still be my Vision, O Ruler of all.

TRADITIONAL GAELIC 8th century A.D.; translated by Mary Elizabeth Byrne, 1905; Versified by Eleanor Hull, 1912 This quintessential St. Patrick's Day hymn takes one of its themes from an ancient *lorica,* a breastplate of Druidic lore that bore an invocation against evil, typical of one that St. Patrick is described as wearing to fend off his foes. The text, *Rob tu mo bhoile, a Comdi cride,* is often attributed to Dallan Forgaill, the chief bard among the Irish, and was part of the Irish monastic tradition for centuries. Mary Elizabeth Byrne, a scholar and translator, produced the first modern prose translation. Eleanor Hull, an influential writer and scholar of Irish history, set it to verse and included it in her *The Poem Book of the Gael.* Hull, president of London's Irish Literary Society, published the seminal *History of Ireland and her People* in 1926.

His Eye Is on the Sparrow

Behold the fowls of the air: for they sow not, neither do they reap, nor gather into barns; yet your heavenly Father feedeth them. Are ye not much better than they? — Matthew 6:26

Why should I feel discouraged,
Why should the shadows come,
Why should my heart be lonely,
And long for heaven and home,
When Jesus is my portion?
My constant friend is He:
His eye is on the sparrow,
And I know He watches me.

I sing because I'm happy,
I sing because I'm free,
For His eye is on the sparrow,
And I know He watches me.

"Let not your heart be troubled,"
His tender word I hear,
And resting on His goodness,
I lose my doubts and fears;
Though by the path He leadeth,
But one step I may see.
His eye is on the sparrow,
And I know He watches me.

I sing because I'm happy,
I sing because I'm free,
For His eye is on the sparrow,
And I know He watches me.

Whenever I am tempted,
Whenever clouds arise,
When songs give place to sighing,
When hope within me dies,
I draw the closer to Him,
From care He sets me free;
His eye is on the sparrow,
And I know He watches me.

I sing because I'm happy,
I sing because I'm free,
For His eye is on the sparrow,
And I know He watches me.

CIVILLA DURFEE MARTIN Elmira, New York, 1905 *Baptist*
Martin found the wellspring of her most powerful hymns in the spiritual strength of the ailing. This, her most famous poem, was inspired by the Doolittle couple, who were each crippled by years of illness. Martin was astonished by their happiness in the face of torturous physical problems, and when she asked about the secret of their joy, Mrs. Doolittle replied, "My heavenly Father watches over each little sparrow and I know he loves and cares for me." Greatly moved, Martin wrote the hymn the night she heard those encouraging words. It has been sung ever since, and has been recorded by many vocalists, including Ethel Waters and Lauryn Hill.

Martin was considered the classic "preacher's wife." Devoted, loyal, and tireless, she used her considerable musical talents in collaboration with her husband's evangelistic work and was more likely his full partner than "helpmate." They collaborated on the writing of gospel songs, including "God Will Take Care of You," written when Martin was herself ill and confined to bed. This simple hymn reportedly gave great comfort to J. C. Penney, who was languishing at a sanitarium when he first heard its words. "I felt as if I had been instantly lifted out of the darkness of a dungeon into a warm, brilliant sunlight. I felt as if I had been transported from hell to Paradise. I felt the power of God as I had never felt it before."

O God of Earth and Altar

Who gave himself for our sins, that he might deliver us from this present evil world, according to the will of God and our Father. —Galatians 1:4

O God of earth and altar,
Bow down and hear our cry,
Our earthly rulers falter,
Our people drift and die;
The walls of gold entomb us,
The swords of scorn divide,
Take not thy thunder from us,
But take away our pride.

From all that terror teaches,
From lies of tongue and pen,
From all the easy speeches
That comfort cruel men,
From sale and profanation
Of honour and the sword,
From sleep and from damnation
Deliver us, good Lord!

Tie in a living tether
The prince and priest and thrall,
Bind all our lives together,
Smite us and save us all;
In ire and exultation
Aflame with faith, and free,
Lift up a living nation,
A single sword to thee.

GILBERT KEITH (G. K.) CHESTERTON London, England, 1906 *Anglican*
The muscular force of this hymn has been used for a century to sway crowds and congregations, to enjoin against the ills of war, unchecked accumulation of wealth, and willful ignorance. Chesterton's rare hymn from his voluminous collection of writings speaks to the author's core beliefs: faith in God's power, mistrust of authority, and the power of the common man. It was written partly in response to England's involvement in the South African Boer War (1899–1902), which he felt was largely inspired by the desire for control of South Africa's diamond and gold resources. Chesterton was a religious apologist all of his life, though he converted from the Anglican Church to Roman Catholicism in 1922.

At 6'4" and 300 pounds, G. K. Chesterton's girth could barely contain his bursting inner life. Best known for his "Father Brown" mysteries, Chesterton was an author, poet, philosopher, essayist, journalist, artist, critic, and historian. In his lifetime he published sixty nine books (at least ten more were published post-humously) and wrote more than 4,000 newspaper articles. He was an exuberant man who counted George Bernard Shaw and H. G. Wells as friends, though he fiercely opposed their views. His own opinions were of some consequence: his book *The Everlasting Man,* reportedly led the atheist C. S. Lewis to Christianity, and a newspaper essay he wrote is said to have influenced the work of Mohandas Gandhi. Although he was considered a reactionary by his peers because of his (temporary) support of Fascism, among other beliefs, his work is now hailed as bold and even prescient by a growing circle of admirers.

Joyful, Joyful, We Adore Thee

My lips will shout for joy when I sing praise to You. — Psalm 71:23

Joyful, joyful, we adore Thee,
God of glory, Lord of love;
Hearts unfold like flowers before Thee,
Opening to the sun above.
Melt the clouds of sin and sadness,
Drive the dark of doubt away,
Giver of immortal gladness,
Fill us with the light of day.

All Thy works with joy surround Thee,
Earth and heaven reflect Thy rays,
Stars and angels sing around Thee,
Center of unbroken praise.
Field and forest, vale and mountain,
Flowery meadow, flashing sea,
Singing bird and flowing fountain
Call us to rejoice in Thee.

Thou art giving and forgiving,
Ever blessing, ever blest,
Well-spring of the joy of living,
Ocean depth of happy rest!
Thou our Father, Christ our Brother,—
All who live in love are Thine;
Teach us how to love each other,
Lift us to the Joy Divine.

Mortals, join the happy chorus
Which the morning stars began;
Father love is reigning o'er us,
Brother love binds man to man.
Ever singing, march we onward,
Victors in the midst of strife,
Joyful music lifts us Sunward
In the triumph song of life.

HENRY VAN DYKE Williamstown, Massachusetts, 1907 *Presbyterian*
Although he wrote more than eighty books and edited many others, Van Dyke was much more than an author. His interests, of which writing was only one, were many and varied: he was also an avid outdoorsman, a well-known professor and critic, a diplomat and ambassador, and a much-loved minister. All of these interests resurface as prominent themes in Van Dyke's later writings, making his literary contributions, including poems, essays, parables, romances, travel journals, and literary criticism, as varied and versatile as his life.

Many of these interests were influenced by his parents and childhood. Van Dyke was born into an old, distinguished family. His father worked as a Presbyterian minister, sparking his son's love for religion and his future career as a minister himself. Henry Van Dyke combined this inherent love for religion with his love for the outdoors and believed that the two, nature and religion, went hand in hand. "Joyful, Joyful, We Adore Thee" is considered by many to be one of the most glorious sacred songs in English. The text was written while Van Dyke was a guest preacher at Williams College. He was evidently pleased with his work, as he offered it to the president of the college, writing, "Here is a hymn for you. Your mountains (the Berkshires) were my inspiration. It must be sung to the tune of Beethoven's 'Hymn to Joy.'" Beethoven, who referred to joy as "the conqueror of grief," in turn had been inspired by Friedrich Schiller's poem "Ode to Joy" when he wrote his Ninth Symphony, from which the music of this hymn is taken.

In Christ There Is No East or West

There is neither Jew nor Greek, there is neither bond nor free, there is neither male nor female: for ye are all one in Christ Jesus. —Galatians 3:28

In Christ there is no East or West
In Him no South or North;
But one great fellowship of Love
Throughout the whole wide earth.

In Him shall true hearts ev'rywhere
Their high communion find;
His service is the golden cord,
Close binding all mankind.

Join hands, then, brothers of the faith,
Whate'er your race may be;
Who serves my Father as a son
Is surely kin to me.

In Christ now meet both East and West,
In Him meet South and North;
All Christly souls are one in Him
Throughout the whole wide earth.

JOHN OXENHAM (William Arthur Dunkerley) London, England, before 1908 *Congregational*
William Arthur Dunkerley gave himself the nom de plume John Oxenham after a character in the book *Westward, Ho*. True to his namesake, Oxenham lived life boldly and fully. He left his native Manchester, England, to pursue a successful business in France, but discovered he loved writing more than the grocery trade. Oxenham returned to England to write full-time; he eventually published scores of novels and poems. His work was known to galvanize and unite a nation at war; in 1917 he was invited to visit the Western Front, an experience that inspired a book of verse and essays. When he was not writing, Oxenham pursued mountain climbing and served as a deacon and teacher at the Euling Congregational Church in London. His daughter, Elsie J. Oxenham, was a best-selling children's author.

"In Christ There Is No East or West" was written as part of the presentation *Pageant of Darkness and Light* for an exhibition sponsored by the London Missionary Society in 1908. Martin Luther King, Jr. inserted quotations from the work into some of his most famous speeches; the hymn was reportedly one of his favorites. Oxenham's words remain deeply relevant a century after their composition.

Will the Circle Be Unbroken?

Then we which are alive and remain shall be caught up together with them in the clouds, to meet the Lord in the air: and so shall we ever be with the Lord. — 1 Thessalonians 4:17

There are loved ones in the glory,
Whose dear forms you often miss;
When you close your earthly story,
Will you join them in their bliss?

Will the circle be unbroken
By and by, by and by?
In a better home awaiting
In the sky, in the sky?

In the joyous days of childhood,
Oft they told of wondrous love,
Pointed to the dying Savior
Now they dwell with Him above.

Will the circle be unbroken
By and by, by and by?
In a better home awaiting
In the sky, in the sky?

You can picture happy gatherings
Round the fireside long ago,
And you think of tearful partings,
When they left you here below.

Will the circle be unbroken
By and by, by and by?
In a better home awaiting
In the sky, in the sky?

One by one their seats were emptied,
One by one they went away;
Here the circle has been broken—
Will it be complete one day?

Will the circle be unbroken
By and by, by and by?
In a better home awaiting
In the sky, in the sky?

ADA RUTH HABERSHON London, England, 1907 *Evangelical*
The author of one of America's most celebrated hymns, the Englishwoman Ada Ruth Habershon has been largely excluded from its glory. Instead, "Will the Circle Be Unbroken?" is commonly attributed to Carter Family patriarch A. P. Carter, who even copyrighted a version of the song in his name. The Carter Family can be credited with making the hymn their own through A. P.'s reworking of the words as well as the strength of their performance, but its creation occurred some twenty years before, in a transatlantic collaboration between a Brit and an Iowan.

Habershon was born in London to a devout Christian family; early in life she turned to evangelical religion. After receiving formal Bible training, she began an intensive study of the Scriptures and authored books on topics including miracles, prophecies, and parables. Key figures were to influence her work, including evangelist Dwight Moody and gospel singer Ira Sankey, with whom she shared lifelong friendships. Habershon collaborated with American composer Charles Gabriel to produce this, her most famous work, a hymn that was to propel the growth of gospel and country music around the nation. The song has since been recorded by more than seventy musical acts, including John Lee Hooker, Tammy Wynette, Joan Baez, Bob Dylan, Gregg Allman, and Willie Nelson.

In the Garden

Jesus saith unto her, Woman, why weepest thou? whom seekest thou? She, supposing him to be the gardener, saith unto him, Sir, if thou have borne him hence, tell me where thou hast laid him, and I will take him away. —John 20:15

I come to the garden alone
While the dew is still on the roses
And the voice I hear falling on my ear
The Son of God discloses.

And He walks with me, and He talks with me,
And He tells me I am His own;
And the joy we share as we tarry there,
None other has ever known.

He speaks, and the sound of His voice
Is so sweet the birds hush their singing,
And the melody that He gave to me
Within my heart is ringing.

And He walks with me, and He talks with me,
And He tells me I am His own;
And the joy we share as we tarry there,
None other has ever known.

I'd stay in the garden with Him
Though the night around me be falling,
But He bids me go; through the voice of woe
His voice to me is calling.

And He walks with me, and He talks with me,
And He tells me I am His own;
And the joy we share as we tarry there,
None other has ever known.

C. AUSTIN MILES Philadelphia, Pennsylvania, 1912 *Methodist*
In 1912, Miles was commissioned by music publisher Adam Geibel to write a hymn that would be "sympathetic in tone, breathing tenderness in every line; one that would bring hope to the hopeless, rest for the weary, and downy pillows to dying beds." Seeking inspiration, Miles randomly opened the Bible to John 20:11–18. Then, in his words, a vision appeared: "I seemed to be standing at the entrance of a garden, looking down a gently winding path, shaded by olive branches. A woman in white, with head bowed, hand clasping her throat, as if to choke back her sobs, walked slowly into the shadows. It was Mary." In this dream state, Miles stood with Mary Magdalene as a witness to the Resurrection of Jesus. When he awoke he recorded his vision as a poem, and wrote the music later that same day.

Following the success of this hymn, Miles gave up a lucrative career as a pharmacist to become an editor and writer. In his words, "It is as a writer of gospel songs I am proud to be known, for in that way I may be of the most use to my Master, whom I serve willingly although not as efficiently as is my desire." Second in popularity only to "The Old Rugged Cross" in evangelical circles, the song was frequently played at Billy Sunday's rallies and services.

O God, I Cried, No Dark Disguise

That they should seek the Lord, if haply they might feel after him, and find him, though he be not far from every one of us:
For in him we live, and move, and have our being; as certain also of your own poets have said, For we are also his offspring.
—Acts 17:27-28

O God, I cried, no dark disguise
Can e'er hereafter hide from me
Thy radiant identity, Thy radiant identity!
I know the path that tells Thy way
Through the cool eve of every day;
God, I can push the grass apart
And lay my finger on Thy heart!

The world stands out on either side
No wider than the heart is wide;
Above the world is stretched the sky,—
No higher than the soul is high.
The heart can push the sea and land
Farther away on either hand;
The soul can split the sky in two,
And let the face of God shine through.

EDNA ST. VINCENT MILLAY Camden, Maine, 1912
Millay was writing poetry by the age of five; her first published poem appeared in *The St. Nicholas Book for Children* in 1906. At her mother's urging, Millay entered a poetry contest in 1912, when she was nineteen years old; she was a Sunday school teacher at the time. "Renascence," a long rhyming poem (of which this hymn is an excerpt), won fourth place and was published in *The Lyric Year,* where it received notice and acclaim. On the poem's merit, Millay was awarded a scholarship to Vassar College. *Renascence and Other Poems,* her first published book and threshold to her fame, was published in 1917. Millay won the Pulitzer Prize for Poetry in 1923, for the book *The Harp Weaver and Other Poems.* She went on to author more than twenty books of poetry, as well as drama and short fiction.

The Prodigal Son

And the son said unto him, Father, I have sinned against heaven, and in thy sight, and am no more worthy to be called thy son. —Luke 15:21

Out in the wilderness wild and drear,
Sadly I've wandered for many a year,
Driven by hunger and filled with fear,
I will arise and go;
Backward with sorrow my steps to trace,
Seeking my heavenly Father's face,
Willing to take but a servant's place,
I will arise and go.

Back to my Father and home,
Back to my Father and home,
I will arise and go
Back to my Father and home.

Why should I perish in dark despair,
Here where there's no one to help or care,
When there is shelter and food to spare?
I will arise and go;
Deeply repenting the wrong I've done,
Worthy no more to be called a son,
Hoping my Father His child may own,
I will arise and go.

Back to my Father and home,
Back to my Father and home,
I will arise and go
Back to my Father and home.

Sweet are the memories that come to me,
Faces of loved ones again I see,
Visions of home where I used to be,
I will arise and go;
Others have gone who had wandered, too,
They were forgiven, were clothed anew,
Why should I linger with home in view?
I will arise and go.

Back to my Father and home,
Back to my Father and home,
I will arise and go
Back to my Father and home.

O that I never had gone astray!
Life was all radiant with hope one day,
Now all its treasures I've thrown away,
Yet I'll arise and go;
Something is saying, "God loves you still,
Tho' you have treated His love so ill,"
I must not wait, for the night grows chill,
I will arise and go.

Back to my Father and home,
Back to my Father and home,
I will arise and go
Back to my Father and home.

THOMAS OBEDIAH CHISHOLM Winona Lake, Indiana, 1914 *Methodist*
Raised in a small town, Chisholm received no formal education, yet became a teacher in a country school at age sixteen, and at twenty-one was named the associate editor of the weekly newspaper, *The Franklin Favorite.* Chisholm became a Christian in 1893. With his minister's encouragement, he moved to Louisville and became the editor of the *Pentecostal Herald,* and was later ordained as a Methodist minister. He was a prodigious poet and hymnist; in his ninety-four years of life, he wrote more than 1,200 poems, of which 800 were published and many of which were set to music. "Great Is Thy Faithfulness," written in 1923, became a standard in Methodist hymnals and the "school hymn" of the Moody Bible Institute in Chicago.

Precious Lord, Take My Hand

In my distress I called upon the Lord, and cried to my God: and he did hear my voice out of his temple, and my cry did enter into his ears. — 2 Samuel 22:7

Precious Lord, take my hand
Lead me on, let me stand,
I am tired, I am weak, I am worn.
Thru the storm, thru the night,
Lead me on to the light.
Take my hand, precious Lord,
Lead me home.

When my way grows drear,
Precious Lord linger near.
When my life is almost gone,
Hear my cry, hear my call,
Hold my hand lest I fall:
Take my hand, precious Lord,
Lead me home.

When the darkness appears
And the night draws near,
And the day is past and gone,
At the river I stand,
Guide my feet, hold my hand.
Take my hand, precious Lord,
Lead me home.

THOMAS ANDREW DORSEY Chicago, Illinois, 1932 *Baptist*
Dorsey's father was an itinerant Baptist preacher; his mother was a music teacher and church organist. Born in rural georgia, he began his career in Chicago after World War I, where he played blues piano under the name "Georgia Tom." A popular act, Dorsey was a regular in one of Al Capone's speakeasies. He married Nettie Harper in 1925, but was soon incapacitated by severe depression. It was during this time that he experienced a spiritual healing. To mark his new life, and after hearing Charles Tindley perform his gospel hymns, he wrote his first gospel song, "If You See My Savior, Tell Him That You Saw Me." In 1932, Dorsey established the Dorsey House of Music in Chicago, the first independent publisher of black gospel music. That same year, he accepted an invitation to become choir director of Chicago's Pilgrim Baptist Church, a position he would hold for nearly forty years. He saw his music as a mission, believing his songs lifted people out of their everyday miseries and gave them hope.

In August 1932, Nettie and their newborn son died within hours of one another. Dorsey was able to find peace through the composition of this hymn. He wrote of the creative experience, "As the Lord gave me these words and melody, He also healed my spirit. I learned that when we are in our deepest grief, when we feel farthest from God, this is when He is closest, and when we are most open to His restoring power. And so I go on living for God willingly and joyfully, until that day comes when He will take me and gently lead me home."

The hymn has become a standard-bearer for peace and hope. Martin Luther King, Jr. asked that it be sung at the rally he led the night before his assassination; President Lyndon B. Johnson requested that it be sung at his funeral.

Now the Silence

Truly my soul waiteth upon God: from him cometh my salvation. —Psalm 62:1

Now the silence Now the peace
Now the empty hands uplifted
Now the kneeling Now the plea
Now the Father's arms in welcome

Now the hearing Now the pow'r
Now the vessel brimmed for pouring
Now the body Now the blood
Now the joyful celebration

Now the wedding Now the songs
Now the heart forgiven leaping
Now the Spirit's visitation
Now the Son's epiphany
Now the Father's blessing
Now Now Now

JAROSLAV VAJDA St. Louis, Missouri, 1969 *Lutheran*
Vajda is a retired Lutheran pastor, and the son of a Lutheran pastor, of Slovak descent. He began translating Slovak poetry at the age of eighteen, but he did not write his first hymn until he was forty-nine. While serving as editor of *This Day* magazine, Vajda faced a moment common in the periodical publishing world: with two days left before going to press, he still had a blank page in the forthcoming issue. While shaving the next morning, he contemplated the eagerness with which both David and Jesus entered the temple for services—and questioned why at times he didn't feel that joy, but went to church more from a sense of duty. He thought about everything that transpired in a single service, any part of which could fill him with wonder and hope. He then wrote this poetic sequence of liturgical events ending in the Holy Trinity—just in time for publication. This hymn has been translated into many languages, including Japanese, Czech, and Chinese.

Vajda's original and translated hymns have appeared in more than sixty five hymnals worldwide; he has also published two collections of hymn texts, numerous books, translations, and articles. He is a fellow of the Hymn Society in the United States and Canada.

As We Gather at Your Table

For where two or three are gathered together in my name, there am I in the midst of them. — Matthew 18:20

As we gather at your table,
as we listen to your word,
help us know, O God, your presence;
let our hearts and minds be stirred.
Nourish us with sacred story
till we claim it as our own;
teach us through this holy banquet
how to make Love's victory known.

Turn our worship into witness
in the sacrament of life;
send us forth to love and serve you,
bringing peace where there is strife.
Give us, Christ, your great compassion
to forgive as you forgave;
may we still behold your image
in the world you died to save.

Gracious Spirit, help us summon
other guests to share that feast
where triumphant Love will welcome
those who had been last and least.
There no more will envy blind us,
nor will pride our peace destroy,
as we join with saints and angels
to repeat the sounding joy.

CARL P. DAW, JR. Storrs, Connecticut, 1989 *Episcopal*
Daw, an Episcopal priest, is the son of a Baptist pastor. A former professor of English, parish priest, and college chaplain, he currently serves as the executive director of the Hymn Society in the United States and Canada. His works have appeared in numerous hymnals from many denominations around the world. This hymn was commissioned by Eastern Shore Chapel in Virginia Beach for the celebration of their 300th anniversary, which used the theme "Repeat the Sounding Joy."

Prayer for Creation

And the bow shall be in the cloud; and I will look upon it, that I may remember the everlasting covenant between God and every living creature of all flesh that is upon the earth. —Genesis 9:16

O Creator of the cosmos, we present our hearts in prayer.
We are awestruck by your glory, which surrounds us everywhere.
From the birdsong of the morning to a stormy sky at night,
You reveal yourself in Nature, in its gentleness and might.

Through each rainbow that you send us you renew your covenant
With the earth and all life on it, telling us of your intent
That each living thing should flourish, in its own way, in its place.
You call us to new awareness of our neighbors and their space.

In our eagerness to prosper, we have ravaged what was good.
Using more than what was needed, taking everything we could.
We have changed the gentle order you intended for the earth.
Now we humbly ask the wisdom to be part of its re-birth.

We seek mercy, we seek vision, and the courage we will need
As we work to help the victims of the sins of human greed.
By our choices, in our actions, may we be part of your plans.
Help us gently till the Garden you've entrusted to our hands.

Finding strength in common purpose, may your faithful people be
Voices for a new perspective, leaders in simplicity.
Give us guidance, O, Creator. Give us power to achieve
True compassion for Creation as the legacy we leave.

CATHY YOST Kirkwood, Missouri, 2000 *Presbyterian*
Yost is an environmental activist within the faith community, having served as the first moderator for the national fellowship Presbyterians for Restoring Creation. In her words, "The desire to care for this planet should be based not only on its preservation for future generations, but also on the fact that the earth and all its creatures, water, and vegetation belong to God. I believe that people of faith are called to be not only the earth's stewards, but leaders in turning around dangerous trends like our unchecked use of finite resources."

The recognition of our responsibility for caring for our planet is increasingly witnessed in the accomplishments of societies like Yost's, and other organizations such as the National Religious Partnership for the Environment, a Judeo-Christian alliance of environmental activists. This hymn was the winning entry in the international Creation Hymn Competition sponsored by the Central Presbyterian Church of Houston, Texas.

Scriptural References Index

All references are quoted from the King James Version of the Bible.

BIBLIOGRAPHY

Numerous sources were referenced in the compilation of this book; the following list includes those most frequently, and most specifically, consulted, and recommended.

BOOKS AND PERIODICALS

Atwan, Robert, and Laurence Wieder, eds. *Chapters into Verse: A Selection of Poetry in English Inspired by the Bible from Genesis through Revelation.* New York: Oxford University Press, 2000.

Bailey, Albert. *The Gospel in Hymns.* New York: Charles Scribner's Sons, 1950.

Barnouw, Eric. *A History of Broadcasting in the United States.* New York: Oxford University Press, 1967.

Beattie, David. *The Romance of Sacred Song.* London: Marshall, Morgan & Scott, 1960.

Bliss, P. P., and Ira D. Sankey. *Gospel Hymns and Sacred Songs.* Biglow & Main, 1875.

Bonomi, Patricia. *Under the Cope of Heaven: Religion, Society, and Politics in Colonial America.* 1986. Reprint, New York: Oxford University Press, 1995.

Bradley, Ian. *The Penguin Book of Hymns.* London: Viking, 1989.

Brooks, Geraldine. "Orpheus at the Plough." *The New Yorker*, 10 January 2005, 58–65.

Brownlie, John. *Hymns of the Early Church.* Grand Rapids, MI: Christian Classics Ethereal Library, 1913.

Campbell, Rev. Duncan. *Hymns and Hymn Makers.* Fourth Edition. London: A. & C. Black, 1908.

Church, Forrest. *The American Creed: A Spiritual and Patriotic Primer.* New York: St. Martin's Press, 2002.

Collins, Ace. *Stories Behind the Hymns That Inspire America.* Grand Rapids, MI: Zondervan, 2003.

Dupont-Summer, Andre. *The Dead Sea Scrolls: A Preliminary Survey.* Oxford: Basil Blackwell, 1952.

Edson, Louis C., ed. *Modern Music and Musicians.* New York: The University Society, 1912.

Eskew, Harry, and Hugh McElrath. *Sing with Understanding.* Second Edition. Nashville: Church Street Press, 1995.

Frawley, Maria. *Anne Brontë.* New York: Twayne Publishers, 1996.

Frost, Maurice, ed. *Historical Companion to Hymns Ancient & Modern.* London: William Clowes & Sons, 1962.

Glover, Raymond F. *The Hymnal 1982 Companion.* New York: The Church Hymnal Corporation, 1990–1993.

Haeussler, Armin. *The Story of Our Hymns.* St. Louis: Eden Publishing House, 1952.

Hallo, William W., and J.J. Van Dijk. *The Exaltation of Inanna.* New Haven, CT: Yale University Press, 1968.

Haynes, Nathaniel S. *History of the Disciples of Christ in Illinois:1819–1914.* Cincinnati: Standard Publishing, 1915.

Heilbut, Anthony. *The Gospel Sound: Good News and Bad Times.* New York: Simon & Schuster, 1971.

Hughes, Charles William. *American Hymns Old and New: Notes on the Hymns and Biographies of the Authors and Composers.* New York: Columbia University Press, 1980.

Hustad, Donald Paul. *Dictionary-Handbook to Hymns for the Living Church.* Carol Stream, IL: Hope Publishing Company, 1978.

Johnson, Guye. *Treasury of Great Hymns and Their Stories.* Greenville, SC: Bob Jones University Press, 1988.

Jones, Ralph H. *Charles Albert Tindley: Prince of Preachers.* Nashville: Abingdon Press, 1982.

Keyte, Hugh, and Andrew Parrott. *The New Oxford Book of Carols.* New York: Oxford University Press, 1992.

Latourette, Kenneth Scott. *A History of the Expansion of Christianity, IV.* Grand Rapids, MI: Zondervan, 1970.

Lewis, C. S. *English Literature in the Sixteenth Century, Excluding Drama.* Oxford: Oxford University Press, 1954.

Mayhew, Kevin, ed. *Complete Anglican Hymns Old and New: Words and Music Edition.* Suffolk, England: Kevin Mayhew, 2000.

Mellers, Willfrid. *Music in a New Found Land: Themes and Developments in the History of American Music.* New York: Oxford University Press, 1987.

Morgan, Robert J. *Then Sings My Soul: 150 of the World's Greatest Hymn Stories.* Nashville: Thomas Nelson Publishers, 2003.

Mouw, Richard J., and Mark A. Noll, eds. *Wonderful Words of Life: Hymns in American Protestant History and Theology.* Grand Rapids, MI: Eerdmans Publishing Company, 2004.

Newman, Richard. *Go Down, Moses.* New York: Clarkson Potter, 1998.

Newton, John and William Cowper. *Olney Hymns.* London: W. Oliver, 1779.

Nutter, Charles S. *Hymns and Hymn Writers of the Church.* Nashville: Smith & Lamar, 1913.

Osbeck, Kenneth W. *101 Hymn Stories.* Grand Rapids, MI: Kregel Publications, 1982.

———. *Amazing Grace: 366 Inspiring Hymn Stories for Daily Devotions.* Grand Rapids, MI: Kregel Publications, 1990.

Patterson, Daniel W. *The Shaker Spiritual.* Mineloa, NY: Dover Publications, 2000.

Putnam, Alfred Porter. *Singers and Songs of the Liberal Faith; Being Selections of Hymns and Other Sacred Poems of the Liberal Church in America.* Boston: Roberts Brothers, 1875.

Reyna, Ruth. *The Concept of Maya: From the Vedas to the 20th Century.* New York: Asia Press, 1962.

Reynolds, William Jensen. *A Survey of Christian Hymnody.* New York: Holt, Rinehart & Winston, 1963.

Routley, Eric. *The English Carol.* New York: Oxford University Press, 1959.

Sablosky, Irving. *What They Heard: Music in America, 1852–1881. From the Pages of Dwight's Journal of Music.* Baton Rouge, LA: Louisiana State University Press, 1986.

Sankey, Ira D. *My Life and the Story of Gospel Hymns.* Philadelphia: P. W. Ziegler, 1906.

Spencer, Jon Michael. *Black Hymnody: A Hymnological History of the African-American Church.* Knoxville, TN: University of Tennessee Press, 1992.

Stulken, Marilyn K. *Hymnal Companion to the Lutheran Book of Worship.* Philadelphia: Fortress Press, 1981.

Van Dyke, Tertius. *Henry van Dyke: A Biography.* New York: Harper & Bros., 1935.

Warren, Gwendolyn Sims. *Everytime I Feel the Spirit.* New York: Henry Holt and Company, 1997.

Watson, J.R. *An Annotated Anthology of Hymns.* New York: Oxford UniversityPress, 2002.

Watts, I., *Hymns and Spiritual Songs in Three Books. I. Collected from the Scriptures. II. Composed on Divine Subjects. III. Prepared for the Lord's Supper.* London: John Lawrence, 1707.

Wesley, John. *Collection of Hymns for the Use of The People Called Methodists.* London: J. Paramore, 1780.

Webber, Robert E., ed. *Music and the Arts in Christian Worship—Book One: The Complete Library of Christian Worship, Volume 4.* Peabody, MA: Hendrickson Publishers, 1995.

Wordsworth, Christopher. *The Holy Year; or, Hymns for Sundays and Holy-days: And Other Occasions.* London: Rivingtons, 1862.

Young, Carlton R. *Companion to The United Methodist Hymnal.* Nashville: Abingdon Press, 1993.

———. *Music of the Heart: John and Charles Wesley on Music and Musicians, an Anthology.* Carol Stream, IL: Hope Publishing Company, 1995.

INTERNET RESOURCES

Anglicans Online. http://anglicansonline.org/special/hymns/.

Bautz, Verlag Traugott. *Biographisch-Bibliographisches Kirchenlexicon* (2004), www.bautz.de/bbkl.

Beavers, Herman. "James Weldon Johnson's Life and Career." *Modern American Poetry,* www.english.uiuc.edu/maps/poets/g_l/johnson/life.html.

Bible.org. www.bible.org/illus.asp?topic_id=1604.

Blue Letter Bible, http://blueletterbible.org/index.html.

The Brontë Parsonage Museum. www.brontë.org.uk/society/7.asp.

Christian Classics Ethereal Library (2005), www.ccel.org.

Christianity Today. www.christianitytoday.com.

Christian History Institute, http://chi.gospelcom.net.

The GK Chesterton Institute For Faith & Culture, http://academic.shu.edu/chesterton/chesterton.htm.

The Cowper and Newton Museum. www.mkheritage.co.uk/cnm/.

Crowe, Kevin. "Full Circle." *eZine* II (July 2004), www.outboundmusic.com/Ezine/Ezine-Fullcircle.asp.

Cyber Hymnal. www.cyberhymnal.org.

The Enchiridion. www.canamus.org/Enchiridion/sourcaz.htm.

"Early American Imprints, Series I. Evans (1639-1800)." *Readex: Archive of Americana.* www.readex.com/scholarl/eai_digi.html.

Falmouth Museums on the Green. www.falmouthhistoricalsociety.org.

Finseth, Ian Frederick. "Liquid Fire Within Me": Language, Self and Society in Transcendentalism and Early Evangelicalism, 1820-1860," http://darwin.clas.virginia.edu/-if2n.

Fries, Adelaide L. "The Moravians in Georgia, 1735–1740." *World Wide School,* www.worldwideschool.org/library/books/hst/northamerican/TheMoraviansinGeorgia/chap4.html.

"From Psalm Book to Hymnal: Selections from the Lowell Mason Collection." Excerpts from an exhibit, January 18 – March 30, 2000, www.library.yale.edu/div/hymnexh.htm.

Gallagher, Susan Van Zanten. "At Home in the Hymn: Early Nineteenth-Century American Women Hymnists." *Susanna: A Literary Journal of Wesleyan Women's Thought*, n.d., www.ptloma.edu/wesleyan/Susanna/Conf/HomeHymn.html.

Guild of Church Musicians. "Vernacular Hymnody and Metrical Psalms (c. 1500 – present)," n.d., www.churchmusicians.org.

Heber, Reginald. "The Gentleman Bishop." *Before Recordings.* The Library of Virginia, n.d., www.lva.lib.va.us/whoweare/exhibits/rootsmusic/before.html.

"Highlander Folk School and 'We Shall Overcome.'" *Music of Social Change.* http://metascholar.org/MOSC/essays/overcome.html.

Hudson, Mike. "Song of History, Song of Freedom." The Roanoke *Times*, January 14, 2001. www.pipeline.com/-rgibson/overcomehistory.html.

Hughes, Peter. "It Came Upon the Midnight Clear." *Dictionary of Unitarian and Universalist Biography*,www.uua.org/uuhs/duub/articles/edmundhamiltonsears.html.

The Hymn Society in the United States and Canada. www.thehymnsociety.org/.

"In Christ There Is No East or West." *Gracenotes*, August 28, 2004. www.sfcentral.org/ministries/music/gracenotes/gn587.html.

Johnson, Susan. Review of Nancy Mitford's *Savage Beauty: The Life of Edna St. Vincent Millay. Working Poet* (February 2001), www.workingpoet.com/reviews/reviews02-02.htm.

Library of Congress. http://catalog.loc.gov/webvoy.htm.

The Literary Encyclopedia. www.litencyc.com/.

Methodist Archives and Research Centre, John Rylands University Library of Manchester, http://rylibweb.man.ac.uk/data1/dg/text/method.html.

New Advent. www.newadvent.org.

National Public Radio. www.npr.org/.

Owens, Lance S., ed. *The Dead Sea Scroll Texts.* Gnostic Society Library. www.gnosis.org/library/psalm.html.

Oremus Hymnal. www.oremus.org/hymnal/.

Palkhivala Nani A. *India's Priceless Heritage, In A Tribute to Hinduism* (2004). In www.atributetohinduism.com.

Poetry.com. www.poetry.com/.

PBS. "Roundtable: Science and Faith." *Evolution* (2001), www.pbs.org/wgbh/evolution/religion/faith/statement_01.html.

Provine, Darren. "Thomas Ken, Bishop and Non-Juror." Darren Provine at Rowan University, 2005, http://elvis.rowan.edu/-kilroy/JEK/03/21.html.

Roger, John. *The Biography of Barton W. Stone.* Cincinnati: J.A. & U.P. James, 1847. In www.lccs.edu/library_archive/hymnals/aux.hstcntxt.php3.

Rosenberg, Jennifer. "Christmas Truce at the World War I Front." *About.com.* http://history1900s.about.com/od/1910s/a/christmastruce.htm.

Siemon-Netto, Uwe. "Luther's Hymns Preserved." *The Washington Times*, December 3, 2004. www.washtimes.com/culture/20041202-111833-7235r.htm.

Sherwood, Grace Hasmann. "The Origin of the Hymns of the Liturgy." *The Catholic World* (January 1944). In Catholic Culture, www.catholicculture.org/docs/doc_view.cfm?recnum=2606.

"Shrine of the Book." The Israel Museum, www.imj.org.il/eng/shrine/research.html.

Smith, Ted, ed. *Publications of the Great War.* Review of "High Altars," by John Oxenham, n.d., www.hellfirecorner.demon.co.uk/review3.htm.

Spencer, Jon Michael. "The Hymnology of Black Methodists." *Theology Today* 46, no. 4 (January 1990), http://theologytoday.ptsem.edu/jan1990/v46-4-article2.html.

"St. Patrick's Lorica." *Irish Culture and Customs*, www.irishcultureandcustoms.com/Poetry/StPatrick.html.

Tindley Temple Ministries. www.gbgm-umc.org/Tindley/history.html.

Website Broadcast Music, Inc.. www.bmi.com/.

INDEX

Richard Krepel's illustrations are created with both traditional and digital collage techniques, using early twentieth-century engravings, wallpaper patterns from antique catalogs, and handpainted papers, among other elements, as source materials. Once the initial design is in place, nuances of color and linework are added in Adobe Photoshop and Corel Painter. Krepel's inspirations include 1930s avant-garde fashion illustration, where sweeping lines play against the shapes of faces, and the architecture, temple art, and poster design he studied while living in India, Vietnam, Singapore, and Thailand.

The title is set in Albertus, a display font designed in 1940 for Monotype Corporation by Berthold Wolpe, a German goldsmith, type designer, and book designer. It was designed at the request of fellow type designer and calligrapher Rudolf Koch, with whom Wolpe apprenticed in London. Albertus is based upon lettering Wolpe chiseled for bronze inscriptions. It is often chosen for religious subjects.

The book is set in Hoefler Text, created for Apple Computers by Jonathan Hoefler. The font design is based upon elements of Linotype Garamond 3. In 2002, The Association Typographique Internationale presented Hoefler with its most prestigious award, the Prix Charles Peignot, for outstanding contributions to type design.